GROWING UP
BRAVE

GROWING UP BRAVE

Expert Strategies for Helping Your Child
Overcome Fear, Stress, and Anxiety

Donna B. Pincus, PhD

LITTLE, BROWN SPARK
New York Boston London

Little, Brown Spark
Hachette Book Group
1290 Avenue of the Americas, New York, NY 10104
littlebrownspark.com

First Edition: August 2012

Little Brown Spark is an imprint of Little, Brown and Company, a division of Hachette Book Group, Inc. The Little, Brown Spark name and logo are trademarks of Hachette Book Group, Inc.

The publisher is not responsible for websites (or their content) that are not owned by the publisher.

The Hachette Speakers Bureau provides a wide range of authors for speaking events. To find out more, go to hachettespeakersbureau.com or call (866) 376-6591.

Library of Congress Cataloging-in-Publication Data

Pincus, Donna.
   Growing up brave : expert strategies for helping your child overcome fear, stress, and anxiety / Donna B. Pincus.
       p. cm.
   Includes bibliographical references and index.
   ISBN 978-0-316-12560-4
   1. Anxiety in children.   2. Fear in children.   3. Stress in children.
4. Parenting.   I. Title.
   BF723.A5P56 2012
   649'. 64—dc23   2011043636

10 9 8 7 6 5

LSC-C

Printed in the United States of America

To my wonderful daughters,
Sarah, Rachel, and Molly,
And to my husband, John, for beginning the adventure

Contents

Contents

Contents

GROWING UP
BRAVE

Introduction

On a warm September evening a couple of years ago, I was scheduled to give a talk to a group of parents and other interested parties on the subject of child anxiety—what causes it and how to prevent it. I hoped for at least a modest turnout. So I was shocked when more than seven hundred people filed into the high school auditorium to hear what I had to say.

Over the course of my two-hour presentation, I provided my audience with information about the nature, proper assessment, and state-of-the-art treatment of childhood anxiety disorders. They asked many questions. I showed video clips of some of my young patients who had successfully overcome their fears and phobias using the techniques I teach children and their parents. What struck me throughout the evening was the surge of emotional responses from parents, caregivers, guidance counselors, school nurses, pediatricians, psychologists, and clergy members. After a round of applause at the end, a line formed in front of my podium. Fifty to sixty people wanted to talk to me about their loved one, their child who suffered from anxiety and who provided the impetus for them to arrive that night in search of answers.

One woman was tearful as she said, "I came here for my granddaughter. She won't go to school. We've had her on medication, but it's not doing much good. Some mornings we have to fight with her just to get her out of bed. It breaks my heart to see her so trapped by her fears and worries." This concerned grandmother said she planned to bring home some of the skills she had learned that evening, and she added, "I only wish I had heard this ten years ago, before things got so bad."

A parent approached to let me know that her daughter was just five years old, but she and her husband arranged for a babysitter so they both could attend and, she hoped, gain some insight into how to encourage her child to "grow up feeling confident and brave." Many family members, this mother said, had what she believed were anxiety disorders and she watched how they had suffered and avoided situations. One refused to fly on airplanes. Another was so timid and fearful that she never seemed to enjoy life. While her young daughter showed no signs of severe anxiety, she stated that she wanted to be "equipped" with ideas and strategies that would help the girl develop coping skills to deal with her emotions as she got older.

One by one, I spoke with people in line. I talked to the father of a preschooler with severe separation anxiety; a mother afraid her children would imitate her own compulsive behaviors; a school nurse who wanted information on what to tell teenagers when they arrived at her office after having a panic attack in the classroom; a teacher wondering how to help her students handle anxiety; a social worker who often saw children she suspected of having underlying anxieties along with behavioral issues; and a pregnant woman who sought help on how not to pass on her vulnerabilities to her yet-to-be-born baby.

Also in line was a young mother who expressed her gratitude for the new skills she had acquired that evening and was determined to put into practice. "I learned so much in just two hours here," she said. "I got some great ideas about how to make some simple changes in our home, so that anxiety never has to become a 'disorder.' It can just be an 'emotion.' You really should write this all in a book!"

The people who came out that September evening, along with the hundreds of other participants in my previous talks and the many families I have worked with directly, provided much of the driving force for my finally sitting down and writing *Growing Up Brave*. The other huge encouragement came from the success stories of children I have helped or witnessed get better after learning basic skills, children and adolescents whose lives were opened up after receiving treatment.

I am the director of the Child and Adolescent Fear and Anxiety Treatment Program at the Center for Anxiety and Related Disorders at Boston University, one of a handful of highly respected specialty centers in the United States that focus primarily on the treatment and study of anxiety. I have spent more than sixteen years treating children and teens for disorders that wreak havoc in their families, disrupt their lives at school, inhibit their ability to make friends, and put them at risk for substance abuse and depression.

What's exciting right now is new research that has led to the development of specific techniques shown to be extremely successful in reducing or eliminating anxiety disorders within the very short time period of one to sixteen sessions. What's even more exciting is the discovery that parents are essential in countering and even in preventing childhood anxiety. This new knowledge offers mothers and fathers a special opportunity to immediately and positively encourage any child, at any age, toward confident, self-sufficient behavior, using effective techniques that anyone can implement anywhere and at any time.

My message is urgent for several reasons.

First, anxiety is the number one mental health disorder affecting Americans today. More than 18 million adults and perhaps as many as one in five children suffer from a diagnosable anxiety disorder, and many others struggle with lower levels of anxiety that nevertheless interfere with their daily lives. For children with consistently excessive fears or worries, there is much at risk. Unchecked anxiety can become debilitating for anyone, but in children it can interfere with critical social and academic development.

Second, in our culture of aggressive medical treatment plans, more children than ever are being prescribed psychotropic drugs to manage behavior. While these medications may be effective in reducing symptoms, they can also cause troubling side effects, and the rush to medicate is in most cases unnecessary.

Third, we want our kids to enjoy carefree childhoods, yet today's academic, social, and cultural pressures have sent anxiety levels soaring, and child psychologists, teachers, pediatricians, and parents are becoming increasingly concerned about the proven significant and negative outcomes for our children and families.

So I am happy to present in this book the good news on how we can approach childhood anxiety. My own research and the work of my colleagues from specialized anxiety centers in the United States and other countries demonstrate that the family environment significantly affects how and if anxiety manifests in children. We begin at such early ages teaching kids to read or to use math concepts, but teaching them how to deal with negative emotions is not usually at the head of the school lesson plan. It is in the interaction between parent and child that kids first and most powerfully learn those critical lessons about life—that it's safe to try new things, that frustration and fear and sadness can be overcome, that situations that make us afraid can be mastered.

Growing Up Brave is divided into several parts. In part I, I will outline the nature of child anxiety disorders, including which fears are absolutely normal and predictable, and which might be a cause for concern. Much of what kids go through is developmentally appropriate, and it is always striking for parents to learn that almost all children can identify at least one fear at each point in their childhood. You will also learn why parenting skills—or parental styles of interaction—can be so crucial in easing high levels of anxiety.

In part II, you'll learn how to set up home and daily routines to include activities that will help your child feel more secure and confident. From learning how to foster a warm attachment to your child through play to establishing a consistent bedtime and sleep procedure, some simple strategies can go a long way toward preventing anxious behaviors from creeping up in the first place.

In part III, you will see how to interrupt spiraling anxiety by helping your child change maladaptive or negative and worrisome thoughts, excessive fearfulness about physical feelings, and avoidant behaviors. Each chapter walks you through the tools you need to bring a child's better coping skills into action. Throughout, you'll read the real-life stories of kids I have worked with in treatment (their identities and case details have been changed), children from preschool age through adolescence who faced crippling anxieties over social situations, difficulty separating from mom or dad, irrational worries about impending disasters, trouble sleeping, and other problems—and you will see how, step by step, they learned to be brave.

Finally, in part IV, I provide some advice to parents whose children might benefit from professional help or medications, and how to go about finding a good therapist.

I am tremendously excited to be able to translate for you years of research executed by myself and my colleagues in the field.

And as a mother, I'm aware that parenting is truly one of the hardest jobs, and knowing how to deal with problems as they arise can be difficult without the right information. That's what you will find here.

Let's get started!

I

UNDERSTANDING CHILDHOOD ANXIETY

CHAPTER 1

The Brave Child

*Learning to Cope with the
Range of Human Emotions*

We all want our children to enjoy a happy, carefree childhood. But that goal can be hard to achieve. From packed schedules and demanding jobs to family complications, economic pressures, illnesses, and on and on, parents today live under a barrage of stressors. So do our kids. Cable television and the Internet deliver a relentless stream of anxiety-provoking news and images into our homes, where impressionable children struggle to make sense of reports about wars, terrorism, violent crimes, environmental disasters.

Then there are the everyday, personal worries and tensions of childhood. Your son has a bossy peer whom he has to sit next to. Your daughter wasn't invited to a birthday party. The first day of kindergarten is looming. A math test is coming up.

Anxiety is real. It's not all bad; in fact, this completely normal human emotion is not only unavoidable, but it's a necessary and useful part of life. Most children figure out how not to let their fears get the better of them. Others have a harder time. And for some, persistent, uncontrolled anxieties make them feel miserable, interfere with age-appropriate development, and cause their parents endless worry and frustration.

In *Growing Up Brave*, I want to share with you this good and hopeful message:

- Children with extreme anxiety or anxiety disorders can get better.
- We are learning more all the time about what helps a child get better.
- Parents—not therapy, not prescription medications—can be the key ingredient in how successfully a child or adolescent begins to approach the world with greater joy and confidence.

In my years as a clinical psychologist working with hundreds of children and families, and in league with other professionals at the forefront of advances in treating anxiety disorders in young people, I have seen again and again the truly life-changing results when parents and children put into practice some relatively simple skills.

Growing Up Brave: What Does It Mean?

A common quick-to-come-to-mind notion is that bravery means not being afraid. "You're afraid of the water? Just jump right in. Get over it. There's nothing to be afraid of! Go ahead. Do it."

Of course, there *are* things to be afraid of. Parents know that, children know that. And some things it's *right* to be afraid of. But kids who are prone to anxiety fear too much, including situations and objects that will bring them no harm.

When I talk about a child growing up brave, I mean one who

over time develops a solid sense of self-efficacy. The psychologist Albert Bandura, sometimes called the father of self-efficacy, writes: "People with high assurance in their capabilities approach difficult tasks as challenges to be mastered rather than as threats to be avoided."[1]

A brave child navigates tough situations, even if he worries that every other kid he knows seems to have no problem with them. He learns to cope with his emotions, no matter what they are or how uncomfortable they make him. He confronts what he's most afraid of, and does not let what's stressful in the world stop him from taking steps, moving forward, and participating in his life. He knows that some things are hard, but even when his brain is saying, *You can't do this*, he develops the personal resources to deal with stress, with daily hassles, and with what frightens him. He learns to be accepting of himself; he feels good about his accomplishments.

That is what you hope to see in your child, the conviction that he can manage whatever comes his way. You play an active role in helping him get there. Part of any parent's job is to encourage a child to feel there's nowhere he can't go—within the context, of course, of teaching what's truly not safe or not appropriate. It's not safe to go off with strangers, but it is safe to walk into the kindergarten classroom even though mom won't be staying with you and you don't know the other kids. You feel worried about going on a playdate, but being a little worried doesn't have to stop you from doing it. You're afraid of the dark and bedtime, but you can sleep and you'll wake up in the morning feeling just fine.

That's what anxious kids want to know. When I work with children, I sometimes ask them what it means to be brave. We talk about who they consider brave people, even among the characters they've met in books and movies. I ask, "What is it about that person that you admire?" Usually, the brave one is identified as being strong. Children tell me, "He can do anything, he's strong, he has a lot of confidence." They say they wish they were more that way themselves.

In gaining self-confidence, with parents' help, children realize that their emotions and sensitivities don't have to derail them from activities that may be a required part of growing up or may just be a lot of fun. And parents can help children learn to go through life without having one eye constantly on what's around the corner or what's ahead. Bravery speaks to the idea of being in the present moment. Anxiety, after all, is a future-oriented emotion. The anxious child is always anticipating, mentally putting himself in an expected situation that he is sure will make him feel just terrible. When you help your child become brave, he discovers that even if you're not around, he has the ability to calm himself, to notice situations and avoid the ones that are not safe and approach the ones that are okay, even if it's difficult.

All this is kind of a tall order, or at least a challenge, for us parents. We're protective. It *hurts* to see your daughter sitting tearfully next to you at the birthday party while all the other little guests are playing musical chairs. It's painful—and maddening or frightening—to watch your son obsessing over routine activities and engaging in compulsive behaviors that may make him seem strange and isolate him from his peers.

The first step in helping your child get control of his emotions is to deal with yours, by appreciating the role of anxiety in life.

Anxiety: A Normal Human Emotion

Anxiety or excessive fearfulness in a child is difficult for parents to confront. We have a hard time with it. We tend to yank our kids back from the situations or objects that are causing them fear, yet we don't react that way with other emotions. If a child is sad, we feel comfortable telling him it's all right, everybody feels sad sometimes, it's okay to cry. If he's angry, well, everybody gets mad sometimes, being angry doesn't mean he's bad or naughty, we just don't hit people.

When a child says he's afraid, our instinct is to wave it off: "There's nothing to be afraid of, don't worry, relax." He talks about having a frightening dream: "It's not real, come on, we'll make some cocoa." He says dogs are scary: "That's all right, you don't have to meet any dogs."

Besides having a tendency to just shoo them away, parents often misinterpret signs of anxiety—the behaviors that worried kids use as coping mechanisms, such as avoidance, physical complaints, crying, tantrums, withdrawal, and clinging—as intrinsic characteristics, "just his personality." Family members, teachers, too, will describe a child as "shy" or say he's "always been a fussy kid" or is "going through a phase."

But fear is normal. In fact, our society has somewhat of a fascination with this emotion. The feelings that are associated with anxiety can be exhilarating. Many children become really excited about Halloween, for example, about all the neat, spooky, ghosty, witchy creatures, and how much fun they are. Kids are intrigued by the anglerfish with the gigantic, scary teeth in the movie *Finding Nemo*. They're thrilled by a roller-coaster ride. Many of us adults actively seek out the sensation of fear. We'll go mountain climbing, skydiving.

So fear and anxiety are natural, part of being human. Sometimes they're actually enjoyable. Sometimes they can be helpful. When I first work with a child, we often start off talking about "emotion identification" (and many children, even older ones, to their detriment, don't possess a "feeling vocabulary"; they don't understand the full range of human emotions). I ask the child to describe the different emotions she experiences. What do they feel like? With older kids, I might say, "Why would I *not* want to take away all your anxiety?"

We discuss the idea that if all her anxiety were eliminated, she wouldn't be safe anymore. She wouldn't know to stop and lurch back when a car came rushing at her. Being afraid of getting hit by a car is obviously what helps her move out of the way. That's what we know as the "fight-or-flight response," which prepares her body to confront the threat and deal with it or to leave the scene as quickly as possible. A little anxiety also enables people to perform better; she can run a bit faster in a competitive race, do a bit better on a test. It can put us on heightened alert in a good way.

The fact that we know certain fears are developmentally appropriate and are experienced across all cultures makes us understand that they are almost hard-wired, or part of the chemistry of the brain. It's adaptive to become afraid of some things; it's how we're supposed to be.

When fears persist, are not age-appropriate, or interfere with daily functioning, however, and when they are undetected, untreated, or misunderstood, a child is at risk in several ways. One teenager's story demonstrates that risk.

When Anxious Feelings Take Over

When 15-year-old Leah came to our clinic for treatment for panic disorder, the girl had just been released from a two-week inpatient program after her parents discovered she'd been skipping school to hang out in the park drinking and smoking pot. In the program, Leah had admitted that she used drugs and alcohol to "numb out" the stress she felt about school and social situations. She told her parents and therapist that simply walking into a classroom would make her heart start to race, and she'd feel so nauseated that she thought she might throw up. She was always afraid of having a panic attack.

Smoking a joint before the day began became a ritual that allowed her to get herself into the school building. At parties, she'd drink heavily in order to lessen her fear that no one would talk to her. She was associating with a group of kids who were making similarly bad choices because she was convinced no one wanted to be friends with her. Leah avoided many social situations out of terror that she'd panic and embarrass herself.

Her mom and dad were shocked to learn how Leah felt. They thought she was just "testing the waters," playing at being an indifferent and rebellious teen. They never considered that their daughter was desperately trying to manage the high levels of anxiety that made her everyday life unbearably stressful.

But in my office that day, Leah told all three of us she couldn't remember ever feeling any other way.

Anxiety and Social Development

Childhood social anxiety tends to become apparent when children first enter social situations. By age three, they are moving away from parallel play (alongside other children with minimal interaction) to social play with peers. They're hard at work developing the skills that allow them to separate psychologically from the caregivers they depend on, growing in autonomy and self-esteem.

Observe in any preschool or playgroup on any day, and you will likely see kids gather in the dress-up areas, assigning roles and costumes: "You be the mom and I'll be the dad and Rachel can be the kitty." They fully inhabit imaginary worlds, learning to adapt to one another's personalities and styles. There is often also a child or two who are reluctant to enter the fantasy play.

They hang back, or seek out the teacher for special attention, or hide in a corner with a picture book.

Such behavior is not always cause for alarm. Some children do hesitate to engage in social play, and there are plenty of boys and girls who feel shy in new situations, or are overwhelmed by kids whose play-style differs from their own. The child who simply has a shy temperament, however, will usually eventually warm to social situations if given time and encouragement.

Leah's mother remembered how her daughter would cling to her when she was a young child, insisting that mom stay during playdates. Although she was chatty and playful at home, Leah refused to go to friends' houses. When she did have friends over to her home, she was sometimes reluctant to play with them unless her mother made an effort to engage both little girls by participating in make-believe games. "Leah loved to be the princess," her mother recalled. "But only if I would join in and be the dragon, or the queen, or whatever extra character she needed." On the rare occasions when mom was successful in initiating shared play between Leah and a friend, and was able to leave the room, it wouldn't be long before the friend came looking for her with the complaint that "Leah won't play unless you do."

If her parents had brought Leah to see me when she was a preschooler, I would have asked them whether Leah found other situations difficult. I would also have asked about the family's nighttime routine. It would not have surprised me to hear that the child insisted on mom or dad sitting with her or even climbing into bed with her until she was asleep. They might have noted that Leah worried excessively that something bad would happen to her or her parents if they weren't all together. And it's likely that during our interview, her mother would have mentioned difficulties with drop-off at school or daily requests to stay home from activities.

These are typical behaviors demonstrated by children with separation anxiety. In our work with adolescents who are diagnosed with panic disorder, we will sometimes hear the teen report having had problems with just these issues as a child.

Leah's parents characterized their young daughter as "a little shy," and they assumed she'd become more outgoing as she got older. They often allowed her to evade situations that distressed her, letting her stay home from birthday parties, for example. The truth was that Leah's anxiety back then was already interfering with her ability to engage with others. Over time, she internalized her parents' message that she was shy, and the more she avoided social encounters and separation situations, the less chance she had to experience success and develop confidence.

Socially anxious children find personal interactions nerve-wracking, whether it's meeting new school classmates or trying to join a group on the playground. Paralyzed by a fear of saying or doing the wrong thing and worried about being disliked, they turn away from the peer interactions necessary to developing a healthy sense of social identity. Consequently, they often fall behind their age-mates in peer relationship skills.

It's understandable that parents might question whether social deficits caused by childhood fears or worries should be of concern during the early years. The fact is, by the time a child begins elementary school, they can emerge as real liabilities.

Anxiety and Academics

If a child carries debilitating anxiety into the school years, she may also face challenges in the classroom.

Studies show that children learn best when they are alert and relaxed, but have trouble storing and retrieving information when excessively stressed. For optimal learning to take place, kids need to be focused and feel safe, and for some anxious kids those two conditions can be impossible to achieve in the classroom environment.

In elementary school, Leah said, she was always terrified that she'd be called on by the teacher, because this meant that the other kids would shift their attention to her. She was afraid to make a mistake, or ask for extra time to figure out an answer. As a result, her earliest classroom memories were of trying to be as unobtrusive as possible. Because all her mental energy was directed at staying invisible, she couldn't concentrate well on anything that was taught.

Teachers recognized that Leah was a bright child from an educated, middle-class family that wanted her to succeed. Despite her anxiety, her work was fine. She was not disruptive, and because she rarely interacted with the other children she was never a source of social drama. Throughout her grade school years, teachers attributed Leah's lack of participation to the fact that she was just quiet.

Next to parents, teachers are on the front lines for identifying troubles. But, quite understandably, they are inclined to focus on children who upset the classroom by being oppositional. They also watch for indications of learning disabilities—delays in communication skills; slow language development; difficulty in forming words, writing, or understanding others; or trouble with spelling, math, and grammar. Students who consistently lose materials, or who do the work but forget to hand it in, may also be on a teacher's radar.

In a busy classroom, with perhaps a couple dozen children to monitor, a teacher might not connect certain behaviors, such as asking to leave the room (by making requests for frequent bathroom passes, for example) or refusing to read aloud, to anxiety. But in fact, the actions of an anxious child can mimic many characteristics associated with learning disorders. She may be so stressed about getting the right answer on a math problem that she attempts to avoid the question altogether, telling the teacher, "I can't do this" or "I don't know." Fears about reading aloud can cause a confident reader to stumble over words or even freeze to the point of being unable to speak. A child who is afraid to go to school may be so distracted in the hours before it begins that she can't organize the materials she needs for the day and consistently leaves homework or notebooks behind.

As parents, we all have expectations for our children's social, academic, and athletic success. We don't often stop to consider that simply by making them attend school, we are requiring them to encounter and cope with potentially stressful events. Many children rise to the challenge, channeling their occasional nerves over tests or sports into sharpened focus and heightened response. But for anxious kids, every day brings the anticipation of inferiority, which reinforces anxiety about performance, which reinforces a reluctance to approach situations. They can begin to engage in extreme avoidance, which can take a dangerous turn in the middle and high school years.

Leah remembered middle school as a horrible experience. She did not fit in with her peers. She still had anxiety over speaking in class, and her reticence was beginning to reflect in her grades. By the late-preteen and early teen years, kids who have not developed age-appropriate social skills are typically excluded from groups and activities. At the same time, teachers may be losing patience with those children whose anxieties interfere with learning, and previously "good students" can find themselves labeled "problem students," especially if they avoid the classroom or are frequently tardy.

Because no one had yet identified Leah's troubles as stemming from extreme anxiety, her parents' insistence that she start to "figure out this stuff" on her own served to reinforce the pattern of inferiority-anxiety-avoidance that had been set in her early school years. They wanted her to "get her act together," go to her classes, and cultivate a "nice group of friends." Leah needed but couldn't ask for their help; she felt her parents were withdrawing from her, while they were convinced that they should practice some "tough love" in order to promote autonomy in their late-blooming daughter. This is by no means an uncommon parent-teen dynamic, and it's not always misguided. But some teens actually need more parental support to develop self-autonomy.

By the time she reached high school, Leah had begun using alcohol in social situations to help her to relax and "fit in" and was smoking pot to "numb out" before classes. She continued to be frightened by the rush of symptoms she felt—the racing heart, the nausea—and worried constantly about having a panic attack. Ultimately, her avoidance techniques led to the chain of events that ended with her visit to my office. She was not that different from a lot of adolescents who find their way to the clinic for treatment.

Reading the Signals

After her initial interview with me, Leah was admitted to the Teen Panic Disorder program. There, she made great progress, in a relatively short space of time, in managing the feelings that had driven her to self-medicate. She learned the coping skills I will present in this book, and by the end of treatment her life had opened up considerably. She was attending school regularly and no longer smoking pot. Hers was a happy ending.

But her story has much to tell us.

When undetected or untreated, excessive anxiety can interfere with development. The parents of young people like Leah are often baffled by what's going on and why their son or daughter is failing to thrive socially and in school. It's also not at all unusual for kids to arrive at my office after having been through a battery of psychological and physical testing in search of answers.

And if, finally, a label like "separation anxiety" or "panic disorder" has been attached to a set of behaviors, the parents blame themselves for misinterpreting the warning signals. One of the most common remarks I hear is, "We didn't know she was so stressed. How did we miss all this? Was there anything we could have done to help her sooner?"

There is much that can be done sooner, and sooner is better than later. Our understandable tendency as parents, as demonstrated by Leah's story, is to shoo away early evidence of anxiety, or deny that there's anything to worry about, or assume it's just a passing phase. Sometimes it is just a passing phase. But many youngsters suffer greatly over insignificant situations. Nipping excessive fears and worries in the bud—through warm, empathetic, and attentive support, and through teaching a child how to deal effectively with negative emotions when they arise— works miracles in preventing small problems from getting bigger. The techniques I explain in *Growing Up Brave* will show you how that's accomplished.

Cognitive Behavioral Therapy

Cognitive Behavioral Therapy (CBT) is a skills-focused approach for combating anxiety. The child and often his parents are taught strategies for examining maladaptive thoughts and changing avoidant behaviors. The techniques are very much hands-on. CBT is not talk therapy, in which the child comes for appointments with a therapist just to discuss his feelings or the events of the week. It is not play therapy, during which a therapist observes how the child is playing and interprets what it means. Many different therapies are available; they're not all bad, but neither are they based on hard evidence of success.

The efficacy of CBT for child anxiety disorders is supported by research. Studies—"randomized controlled trials," as they are called—have shown that the majority of children who receive CBT are diagnosis-free or much improved after treatment and tend to maintain their gains. That's important data. It's why this is considered the state-of-the-art intervention, the gold standard treatment for anxiety disorders.

My work includes the development of cognitive behavioral treatments for youth with anxiety disorders, and the dissemination of these procedures to therapists and others who work with troubled kids. But I also want to get the information out to parents, and part of that message is that not all children need therapy. (In chapters 2 and 11, I outline the behavioral signs and signals that suggest a child can benefit from professional therapy.) In fact, most kids who show symptoms of anxiety just need to learn a few CBT-based skills. Some of these skills are ones that parents can teach.

Research has demonstrated that, invariably, a child's anxious response to a situation or object he fears can be deconstructed or broken down into separate parts. We call this the "cycle of anxiety," the interrelated influences of thoughts, feelings, and behaviors. When your child is afraid or worried, what behaviors do you see? What thoughts are on your child's mind, and what physical sensations does he experience? I will show you how to plug these observations into the cycle so that you can start to see why he's having the problems he's having.

Once you understand your child, you can begin to figure out

how to help by breaking the cycle. That might mean encouraging him to replace his worrisome thoughts with ones that are more realistic, or to develop the more accurate perceptions that lead to a healthier way of coping. It might mean showing him how to gain control over his physiological reactions to stressful events by learning to "ride the wave" of anxiety until his body calms down. It means helping him take small steps, one at a time, to change behaviors from avoiding or resisting situations to entering them with new courage.

These strengths and competencies will enable him to approach difficult tasks as challenges to be mastered rather than as threats to be avoided. He will build up a kind of toolbox of life skills. I like to think about teaching skills as inserting protective factors, buffering a child from the predictable stresses of the world and from the possible vulnerabilities of his nature and circumstances.

Skills-based treatment requires some motivation on a child's part (and on that of his parents), but what I have learned in years of working with children and teens is that every fearful child wants to feel better. Every child wants to learn to be stronger.

I gave this book the title *Growing Up Brave* (and not, perhaps, *Helping Your Child with Anxiety*) to emphasize the bigger picture of the lessons it describes. You are involved in your child's developmental stages. You are fostering a lifetime of confidence.

CHAPTER 2

What's Normal, What's Not

*Decoding Childhood Emotions,
Fears, and Anxieties*

At a recent birthday party for my daughter's friend, I was standing with a group of parents, watching the children dig into the carrot cupcakes with the abandon of 4-year-olds. Some crammed whole cupcakes into their mouths, others broke off tiny pieces and nibbled at them cautiously. One little girl glanced furtively at her mom as she carefully licked off the white icing.

"Aren't you going to try the cupcake?" her mother prodded.

The little girl shook her head emphatically: no!

"Try a taste, honey. It's good," the mother urged.

"I don't want to," her daughter said.

Mom pointed to the other kids demolishing their cake in a flurry of crumbs and smeared frosting. "Why don't you give it a try?"

Her daughter pushed away from the table so violently that her chair fell over. She began to cry and insist that she wanted to go home right away.

The mom turned to me in exasperation. "She will only eat

things that are white," she said. "Please tell me this is just a stage, not the beginning of a food phobia or eating disorder."

A seemingly innocuous behavior on the part of a very young child had burgeoned in this mother's thoughts into the seeds of a major problem. I hear these parental worries whenever I give a talk or run a workshop. I am invariably questioned by parents as to whether a child's behaviors are age-appropriate quirks or sign-posts of deeper troubles. They ask:

"My 3-year-old only wants dino-shaped chicken nuggets and hot dogs. Is that normal?"

"My 7-year-old daughter is resistant to wearing anything that isn't blue, and she can't stand tags or buttons on her clothing. Should I be concerned?"

"My 10-year-old needs constant reassurance that we'll be okay when her dad and I go out at night. If we deviate from our plan or we're late, she becomes agitated. Is this normal?"

"My 8-year-old still wants to sleep with a night-light. Should I let her?"

"My 12-year-old Little Leaguer has more pregame routines than a major leaguer. Should I try to break some of his habits?"

"My teenager can't sleep the night before an exam, and it's hurting his grades. How can I get him to just relax?"

Is it normal? What can I do?

The bottom line is that we all—adults and children—are sometimes stressed and anxious. When it comes to common childhood fears and anxieties, it is helpful and encouraging to understand that they tend to follow a particular sequence and result in specific behaviors from infancy to adolescence. And many of these fears disappear by themselves over time.

It's normal for a 3- or 4-year-old to be afraid of the dark. A 6-year-old who is unnerved by the loud sounds and flashing lightning of a severe storm is probably working through a pre-dictable developmental stage. A teenager who gets sweaty palms when speaking in front of her class for the first time is experiencing a reasonable level of stress, one common to many adolescents.

On the other hand, an 8-year-old who can't sleep without a night-light and a parent present is more likely suffering from underlying worries and finds nighttime stressful. A 10-year-old who thinks that every strong wind means a tornado is imminent and who refuses to venture out in the rain is exhibiting heightened fears. The teenager who feels she needs to drink alcohol to "loosen up" at a party may be trying to cope with overwhelming anxiety.

In this chapter, we will look at what's normal and what's not. In talking about "what's not," I outline and illustrate the six most prevalent anxiety disorders experienced by children and adolescents. I hope you will use this broad spectrum of behaviors to help you recognize when your child's fears are par for the course and when some attentive interaction on your part is needed.

But first, where does anxiety come from?

Anxiety: What Causes It?

The mother of a child brought in for therapy said she'd been thinking about this whole matter of anxiety and whether it ran in her family. She decided it did. "Practically everyone on my side, and that includes me, is a nervous Nellie. One of my uncles—this is many years ago—I think suffered a nervous breakdown, though nobody talked about it. My mother worried about everything, to the point that we couldn't leave the house without checking ten times that the stove was off, the back door was locked, et cetera, et cetera. My older sister practically wouldn't let her two kids out of her sight until, when they got to be teenagers, they pretty much told her to back off and leave them alone."

Were anxious tendencies inherited, she wanted to know? Was she responsible for the fact that her son was afraid to take part in normal kid activities, like going to parties and other events, seemed to worry a lot, and consequently just didn't seem to be having much fun?

This mom raised a legitimate question, one I've heard many times. Research does show that the vulnerability to experience anxiety disorders may be heritable. A child's temperament or personality—whether she's inclined to be withdrawn or inhibited, for example—will be partly determined by genes. That's not enough to produce a particular disorder, but the predisposition, the genetic loading, will likely make the child more sensitive than others to a certain degree of stress in the environment. Yet even if it's "in the genes" on both sides of the family, it doesn't necessarily mean the child will develop a disorder. (Dr. David Barlow, a leader in the field, writes extensively about the causes of anxiety in his book *Anxiety and Its Disorders*.)[2]

Many influences come into play. Seeing disturbing images or stories on TV can make children fearful. Fear might develop after a child has gone through some form of trauma. We know that major life events can be difficult for some kids to navigate. Many studies talk about children of divorce, for example, and the main stressors that children experience around this event. Other situational issues—moving to a new city, a parent losing a job, changing a nanny—can have an impact. Some kids handle them just fine; they're resilient. Others need extra support.

I reassured this "nervous" parent that although her child might have a genetic vulnerability, it is not likely that she simply "gave" an anxiety disorder to her son, despite the family history.

More to the point, and even more reassuring, with small adjustments in how she probably interacted with her child, it was in her power to make an enormous difference in easing the youngster's fearfulness and timidity. For example, she could model better or non-nervous behavior (more about this in chapter 3). Children do watch us. They pick up cues about what's a worry and what's not a worry from the way we behave.

In fact, the burgeoning field of cognitive neuroscience is coming up, practically on a monthly basis, with indications that experience can influence the expression of genes, or how certain genes are switched on or off. Psychologists are starting to connect some of this research with the kind of applied research that I do, such as understanding how certain cognitive-behavioral skills actually affect a child's brain. Even if a youngster has been genetically loaded for anxiety, the right kind of parental interaction on a regular basis may be able to reinforce desirable pathways in the brain and discourage other, less desirable pathways.

Instead of worrying about what causes a child's anxiety, we parents can better focus on what we can, normally, expect. The following guidelines describe common fears at the different stages of childhood.

Ages and Stages: The Normal Fears of Childhood

Ninety percent of all children, ages 2 to 14, tell us they have at least one fear; many report more than one. We say that in early childhood, kids' fears can change pretty frequently. And most children, across cultures, go through a common trajectory of fears at predictable stages, a progression that largely follows cognitive development—the increasing ability to think about what's real and what's not, about what one can see and can't see, about the past and present and future. The progression follows a general course from the more concrete to the more abstract.

Especially during the younger years, the fears that arise naturally are adaptive mechanisms; they're meant to protect. At different stages, your child is afraid of something that, if not controlled, might affect his survival, or in other words, might cause him to be hurt. So your baby clings to you in alarm if a stranger tries to hold him. The toddler shrinks back when he sees a spider, not knowing whether or not this creature poses a danger.

What we understand about these fears is that just as they surface at particular times they also tend to dissipate with development. Your spider-spooked youngster six months later will let you know he's over that.

While none of these age-specific anxieties is etched in stone — there's a good deal of variability as to when or whether they will appear, depending on temperament, life circumstances, wide ranges in developmental milestones, and a variety of other factors — here's the generally accepted schedule:

Infants and Toddlers

- **Loud noises**

Drop a large pot in your kitchen, and your baby will likely shriek in fright. She doesn't know if the racket means danger.

- **Large or unfamiliar objects**

Because your young child has no basis on which to judge whether unfamiliar things are going to be dangerous, her brain tells her, *Okay, just to be safe, let's turn on the anxiety system in case this is a problem.*

When I blew bubbles out of the toy wand toward my 1-year-old, who'd never seen bubbles before, she began screaming, as though I'd just loosed daggers into the room. Although she's an easygoing, not overly sensitive child, she was clearly terribly scared. I sat her on my lap, so she was on the other side of the bubbles, let her touch the bottle, and showed her how to gently blow a bubble. Then I smiled as I popped the bubbles with my finger, one by one. Gradually, she quieted down.

- **Strangers**

Your 3- or 4-month-old doesn't start crying when she sees someone she doesn't know. When, a few months later, her sight becomes more developed and she gains the ability to differentiate familiar from unfamiliar faces, she may develop stranger anxiety.

This, again, is a protective mechanism. It's not abnormal for your 7- or 8-month-old child to cry when the pediatrician wants to pick her up, though at your previous well-baby checkup she was fine with it. It doesn't mean she is anxious; she understands she shouldn't go with someone she doesn't know. It's adaptive, keeping her close to her caregiver.

Hold your youngster in your arms as you're chatting with a neighbor, and your child will be content. Let the neighbor, being friendly, arms outstretched, say, "Come here, sweetie, let me give you a kiss," and you will likely feel your child resist, her grip tightening. She turns her head away, or starts to whimper.

Usually anxiety over unfamiliar faces resolves around the end of the first year.

Preschoolers, Ages 3 to 5

- **Costumed characters, monsters, ghosts**

As a child's world expands, he begins trying out new situations and testing the world. Between ages 3 to 5 or 6, your child is figuring out what's real and what isn't. You may see him having trouble with the clown or the magician wearing a mask: *Why is that person's face like that? Why are his eyes not moving? If it's a real person, why is it pretending to be not real?* Things not functioning the way he knows real things do is upsetting.

Ghosts, monsters, anything supernatural, might be scary. Younger preschoolers, especially, have these fears. By ages 5 and 6, they're getting a better handle on the whole matter of pretend creatures and imaginary dangers.

- **Fear of the dark and sleeping alone**

Preschoolers might also struggle with fear of the dark, of the basement, of what's under the bed or in the closet. Most kids naturally and gradually realize there's nothing to frighten them, and with the proper parent encouragement, they can sleep alone. Others have more trouble, and this is when many sleep problems arise and when fear of the dark can expand into difficulties with the whole nighttime family routine.

- **Other specific fears**

Many children at this age develop specific fears—about dogs, insects, water, blood, elevators. The fear may connect to a sense of being out of control because of limited knowledge: *Which dogs do I need to be afraid of? Or do I need to be afraid of all of them?* And it may connect to observing the reactions of others: *Why does Mom jump when she sees a bug? Is this really scary or not?*

- **Separation anxiety**

Children grow a healthy attachment to their parents or primary caregivers, the critical developmental task that begins in infancy and continues through preschool and the early childhood years. Separation anxiety, or fearfulness at leaving a parent, can appear in infancy and usually dissipates gradually, but it can resurface at school entry. The youngster heads into preschool, mom or dad starts to head out the door, and crying and clinging ensue. It usually lessens over the next two or three years, and by the end of kindergarten most kids have mastered the idea of separating, knowing that a parent is coming back again.

Awareness of death and dying usually develops around this time; many children learn about it through their religion. In the context of separation anxiety, it's not unusual for a child to express fears about a parent dying.

My older daughter has asked me, "Are you old? Does that mean you're going to die before me? Is Grandma going to die before you? What happens when you die? Where do you go?" That's normal. I try to answer her as simply and honestly as I can.

Though we tend to expect separation anxiety within this time frame, it isn't necessarily a problem if it's still lingering at age 4 or 5. It is even normal for kids this age to have trouble separating initially when starting a new activity. Usually with some practice or after a few tries, the separation gets easier.

Early School Age, Ages 6 to 10

- **Social pressures**

Developing peer relationships is a major challenge. Children at this age have access to many sources of new information, through the Internet and elsewhere, and are trying to sort out images and ideas that have an impact on their social interactions, what other kids know or have and how they fit in. It's terribly important to some children that they find a best friend. They can feel lonely and different without one, or if a friend moves away.

- **Real-world dangers**

At this stage, children fear burglars, kidnapping, storms, lightning, illness, bodily injury. They have trouble distinguishing between a remote risk and an imminent danger and have concern over being and staying safe. They may worry about getting sick.

- **Death in the family**

The possibility of a loved one dying becomes less of an abstraction. A child may repeatedly seek reassurance from a parent that mom or dad is feeling all right, taking care of his or her health, not going anywhere.

- **School failure**

Many children start to worry more than they did before about doing well in school, getting good grades, and pleasing their parents and teachers. They may take even a temporary failure hard.

Middle School Age, Ages 10 to 13

- **Social status**

By middle school, many children become concerned with social status. Your child starts comparing herself to her peers; she worries, will I be accepted, am I smart enough, am I pretty enough?

- **Making and keeping friends, avoiding enemies**

The social cliques and informal groups of middle school can be a source of torment for a lot of kids. Many teens and young adults, in retrospect, describe middle school as the worst time of their life. Kids are afraid of getting bullied. Relational aggression—intentionally rejecting and isolating a classmate—can create misery.

- **Academic and athletic performance**

Sports are often a major aspect of middle school, high school, life. Kids worry about performing well, living up to their own and others' standards, or not letting the team down. In the classroom, a child is usually expected to be more of a participant than in earlier years, to offer ideas and volunteer interpretations, which can be stressful.

Adolescence

- **Sexuality and body image**

Young teens focus intently on their physical selves. They may fear they're not "normal" in some way, and they may be uncomfortable talking to anyone, especially parents, about their fears.

• **Social relationships**

While many kids at this time begin pairing off with romantic partners, the child who is unattached can worry about her place in the peer community. Informal groups are still a big part of social life, and teens fear being left out, having no one to "hang" with.

• **The future, careers**

As pressures increase to do well on test scores and get accepted to a good college or find a job, many kids cope with fears about the future. Life is getting more real and more serious. It can be a little scary, though exciting, to be leaving childhood behind.

• **Moral issues**

Adolescents often start to concern themselves with the larger world. They may brood about injustices, inequalities, matters of right and wrong.

Red Flags: When Should You Become Concerned?

What's important is not necessarily the content of the fear or worry, but how extensively it's interfering with your child's functioning or affecting the atmosphere of family life. He might not talk about the thing that's bothering him, or even recognize what it is, but several signs offer clues that it's probably time to give him added attention (I'll tell you just how to do that in parts II and III), or perhaps even to get outside help from a therapist.

It's appropriate to become concerned if:

• your child's worry lasts for months at a time, and is causing obvious physical distress, such as headaches, upset stomachs, nightmares, and trouble going to sleep.

• he's persistently refusing to go to school, or you learn he has trouble concentrating in the classroom.

(continued)

- he seems unusually gloomy and pessimistic, and indulges in catastrophic thinking (if this or that happens, it's going to be the end of the world).
- he asks for a lot of reassurances (Am I going to be okay? When are you coming home? Will you call me? Will you go with me? Will you tell me you love me three times before I have to go to bed?).
- he becomes anxious and upset if the reassurances are not coming or don't last long enough or cover enough ground.
- he seems often irritable and angry, perhaps out of frustration with himself or perhaps because he's so sleep-deprived that he's simply worn out.
- he asks a lot of "what if?" questions, and answering his questions two or three or five times doesn't seem to calm him down.
- he is excessively self-critical; nothing that he does, he believes, is ever good enough.
- he's excessively concerned about what others think of him.
- he persistently avoids participating in expected activities with peers, such as going to parties or friends' houses, and says he'd rather stay home than go to a family gathering or to church or temple.
- he talks about suicide or says he wishes he were never born.
- his fear is significantly interfering with your family life.

It's wise to become concerned if you realize you're spending more of your time and mental and emotional energy on *any* of these issues than simply on enjoying and having fun with your child.

Anxiety Disorders of Childhood and Adolescence

Fear seems to be intrinsic to development, a natural response to a perceived threat or difficulty, as the list of "Ages and Stages" fears demonstrates. The child responds with avoidance, perhaps, some cognitive distress (worry thoughts), some physical arousal (sweaty palms, rapidly beating heart). Typically, all that goes away on its own, without the child or her parents having to do anything about it.

When normal fears don't go away on their own, we may see a child with a phobia, an exaggerated, persistent, and disturbing fear—beyond the bounds of what constitutes a true threat—that results in maladaptive behavior. We may see a child with excessive, disabling anxiety, or apprehension without apparent cause. The child isn't sure precisely what to expect, but she knows that whatever is coming at her won't be good.

Anxiety disorders appear on the far end of the "normal" continuum. Everyday worries are normal; generalized anxiety disorder is not. Harmless superstitions are normal; obsessive-compulsive disorder is not. A little clinginess is at one end of the continuum; separation anxiety disorder is at the other end. A little shyness is at one end; social phobia is at the other end. The child experiences fear that is probably interfering with aspects of her functioning—academic, social, and family.

A discussion of the different anxiety disorders follows.

Separation Anxiety Disorder

Separation anxiety, or fearfulness about leaving a parent or caregiver, typically peaks during the first and second years, and decreases after that, although it's fairly normal during preschool and early childhood when kids have to separate for the first time to join structured peer groups. If it is accompanied by somatic complaints such as stomachaches, occurs frequently in numerous situations, and causes the child distress or impairs her ability to be away from her caregiver, some intervention is necessary. A youngster with separation anxiety usually worries excessively about something bad happening to her (what if she gets sick at school and mom isn't there?) or to her parent (mom or dad will be in a car accident).

From toddlerhood on, 8-year-old Hannah had great difficulty being apart from her parents, especially her mother. Though both parents had jobs they went to every day, during preschool, kindergarten, and first and second grades Hannah insisted that one of her parents, and not a nanny or babysitter, be the one to drop her off at school and pick her up after. This was obviously an inconvenience for mom and dad, but if they didn't comply the girl cried or even had a tantrum and had to skip school that day.

Her mother remembered the first day of preschool, when Hannah was 2½. "Several of the children were kind of fussy and fretful," she said. "Then this very sweet young teacher started talking gently, and she did that little game with her fingers, 'The itsy-bitsy spider went up the water spout.' The children were delighted, except for Hannah. She stayed glued to me. She started to cry. That was a sign of things to come. It never really got much better."

Hannah's separation anxiety had turned into a liability by the time I met with her and her family. Recently, she had been invited to a classmate's house after school. While there, she had the classmate's parent place three phone calls to her mom at work. Hannah told her mom that she wanted to hear her voice, and she asked if her mother was okay. The invitation to the classmate's house was not repeated.

"It seems she can't let me out of her sight," said Hannah's mother. "She even tags after me around the house."

Generalized Anxiety Disorder

If a child experiences chronic, excessive, and unrealistic worry about multiple areas of life, if his imagination runs wild with all the bad things that might happen and he can't seem to turn it off, or if he spends a lot of time brooding over past conversations or actions, that's generalized anxiety disorder (GAD). We consider that diagnosis if the excessive worrying has gone on during most days for a period of at least six months. The child is tense, keyed up or on edge, always waiting for the other shoe to drop. He, too, might experience stomachaches, headaches, or sleep disturbance. Other symptoms might be constant fatigue, difficulty concentrating, irritability, and muscle tension.

Eddie, a 9-year-old, was a bright and engaging child, described by many adults who met him as "just the nicest little boy." He had friends; he had several interests, including a growing fascination with performing magic tricks. He liked school well enough. But Eddie was constantly and increasingly distracted by worrying — about everything, all day long.

He worried about his grades, about the possibility of a bomb attack, and about what time his father would be home from work. When his family was planning a summer vacation, he wanted to know: Suppose it rains? What will we do then? What if somebody gets sick? Will we be able to get to a doctor or a hospital? When his parents were talking about moving into a bigger apartment in their building, he asked if they could afford it. Did they have enough money? What if Dad lost his job? Would they be able to move back into their smaller, less expensive apartment?

His mother and father called Eddie "the house policeman." He bombarded them with worry questions, which they answered sensibly, patiently, and reassuringly, though they admitted they were getting pretty tired of the whole routine. They viewed their son with some bemusement, some concern, but mostly wished he would just ease up and relax.

Specific Phobias

Children of all ages may display specific phobias, or intense and irrational fears of particular objects or situations. The trigger may be animals, heights, enclosed spaces, vomiting, germs, injections, elevators, and so on. The child may not realize that being afraid of an elevator is unreasonable. Exposure to the trigger produces an anxious response, such as screaming, crying, freezing, or clinging, and often scary physical sensations, like dizziness or rapid heart rate. What would be considered a normal reaction in a toddler can become a serious disorder in an older child, when the fearfulness persists over time and interferes with normal living.

Lyndsey, age 10, had a phobia about dogs that began several years earlier. When she was 5 and sitting around the table at a family dinner, she listened to her grandfather talking about a boy he knew growing up. Grandpa and the friend lived in the same neighborhood, and one day walking home from school, they passed a house with a large dog loose in the yard. The boys stayed at a distance, near the curb. When they were almost beyond the house, the dog leaped over the fence and attacked the friend from behind. "Ripped his ear clean off," Grandpa said. "Buddy started screaming, blood everywhere. I picked up his ear off the ground and we lit out of there." These days, the grandfather mused, "They'd probably be able to sew it back on. But Buddy just had this little twisted stump where his ear used to be."

Lyndsey's intense fear of dogs meant any outing was nearly impossible. The sight of a dog even at some distance caused her heart to pound, and that symptom brought on even further distress. The circumstances of her phobia demonstrate that a child doesn't necessarily have to experience a one-on-one encounter with the feared situation or object. Lyndsey's mental image of a fierce dog and a torn-off ear was enough to initiate her response.

Some kids will develop a specific phobia after seeing a friend or sibling under attack, even if the friend or sibling does not react phobically.

Obsessive-Compulsive Disorder

We all entertain some superstitions. As kids, we may have picked up, and acted on, that old saying, "Step on a crack, break your mother's back." Many athletes have their superstitious habits; the baseball player has to touch his cap a certain number of times before coming to bat, the bowler has to do a certain number of chalk wipes on his hands. Many children have little routines, repetitive actions they like to perform, to comfort themselves and help bring a sense of order and control to their world.

When a child has unwanted, disturbing, and persistent thoughts, impulses, or images (obsessions) that occupy his mind, he may develop repeated behaviors (compulsions) to alleviate his anxiety. Common obsessions are thoughts about contamination, doubting oneself, needing to have things in a particular order, aggressive impulses, or fear of a parent's death or disease. The child tries to neutralize these disturbing images with some other thought or action. Typical compulsions are hand washing, arranging, checking, counting, tapping or touching, and repeating words silently. OCD usually appears in childhood or adolescence. The repetitive behaviors are not pleasurable to the child and are time-consuming, but he's driven to perform them to reduce his discomfort or to prevent some imagined event from occurring. Stopping compulsions usually causes him great distress.

Compulsive behaviors seem to have no logical connection to the real world. They result from a kind of magical thinking that makes no sense to anyone else. One boy believed that it was necessary for him to apply fifteen swipes of deodorant under each arm before he left home in the morning, or a terrible harm would come to his family. One girl had to jiggle a doorknob back and forth eight times before entering any closed room, or she feared she wouldn't be successful in her life.

Edie, a sweet and gentle fifth grader, developed, her mother said, "All these little compulsions about doing her schoolwork and just keeping her room in a certain way. If she didn't do things in a certain order, she would make herself kind of crazy." Before she could start any assignment, Edie had to line up pencils and notepaper in a particular pattern on her desk. Before she left for school in the morning, she checked to see that her shoes were arranged on her closet floor the way she wanted them. "If I moved anything around, like her shoes," her mother said, "she'd know it immediately and have a fit."

Edie would never do her homework anywhere but in her room—not at the kitchen table, never at a classmate's house. She wanted no one near her. Her mother, becoming concerned about what she saw as Edie's "rigidity and this need for perfection," made a point one early evening of being in the girl's room while she worked. Edie was typing a book report on her computer, and her mom noticed that her daughter typed a number of periods at the end of every sentence, then deleted all but one. "I asked her about it," the mother said, "and Edie said she had to do seven periods and erase six of them. I asked her why, and she said it was just what she had to do. She didn't want to talk about it anymore."

Panic Disorder

Most of us have had a panic attack at some point, intense fear and unease composed of both physical symptoms and anxious thoughts. During a scary or powerfully distressing moment, we've felt our heart racing, had difficulty catching our breath or numbness or tingling in the limbs. We may have thought we were going crazy or were stuck in some kind of an unreal or dreamlike state. The symptoms accelerated quickly, peaked after several minutes, and then diminished either rapidly or gradually. When the moment passed, we were not overly concerned; we didn't worry about those sensations coming back.

The child who develops a panic disorder, however, experiences repeated panic attacks and a persistent worry over the recurrence of an attack. Even thinking about it can produce trembling, nausea, heart palpitations, or dizziness. She will try to avoid situations that she thinks might bring them on, or she'll endure those situations with great mental and physical distress.

Panic disorder typically does not occur until adolescence, though a younger child might have an isolated panic attack.

When she was 13, Jessica had a bad cold. At one point she coughed up some phlegm and thought for a second she was choking. She was fine, recovered from her cold, and returned to her normal activities. Soon, however, she began to feel that her throat was closing and she couldn't catch her breath. These symptoms began each evening when she went to bed, until one night she woke her parents by screaming that she couldn't breathe. Her alarmed mom and dad rushed her to the emergency room. A workup determined that she wasn't having an asthma attack, the first line of suspicion. A later visit to the family doctor showed no evidence of allergies. More medical tests were conducted; all results were negative. Jessica seemed to be perfectly healthy.

Her fearful thoughts, however, were taking over. Every night before she went to bed, she asked her parents, "Am I going to stop breathing? Will I be okay tomorrow? Will I get a funny feeling in my stomach?" She insisted they answer the questions sequentially, and if they didn't, she began crying. During the day in school, Jessica was half concentrating on the classroom work, half worrying she would have another attack. As soon as she felt, or thought she felt, a little tightness in her throat, her heart began pounding. She believed she was dying. On a few occasions, she left the classroom. Over several months, Jessica dropped out of all activities that she had previously enjoyed, including dance lessons. Constantly worried about the onset of her symptoms, she avoided as much of her life as she could.

Social Phobia

Some children are more shy and some are more outgoing, and that's what makes the world go round. Having a shy temperament is not abnormal. In fact, kids who are shy may be uneasy around others, but they don't necessarily stay away from situations that make them uncomfortable. Social phobia, on the other hand, is at the far end of the spectrum, characterized by an intense fear of becoming humiliated or embarrassed in social situations. Disrupting a child's normal life and interfering with school and relationships, it often begins around adolescence or during preadolescence, as soon as kids become aware that others are looking at them and making decisions, good or bad, about what they see. A key complaint reported by many youngsters is a terror of appearing foolish or doing something that would invite ridicule from peers or authority figures.

We distinguish between performance-type social phobia, such as excruciating difficulty speaking in public or reading aloud in front of the class or eating and drinking with others around, and generalized social phobia, which causes a child anxiety in many interpersonal situations. She might have trouble even making eye contact with other people.

Alice was a girl who enjoyed an essentially sheltered life for her first 12 years. Her family was close-knit. She lived with her parents, brother, and grandparents in a roomy apartment in the city, where Alice spent cozy afternoons watching soap operas on TV with her grandma—her parents both worked outside the home—or indulging in her favorite pastime, reading. She attended a small parochial school with a strict academic regimen that suited her quiet and diligent nature. She was one of nine students in her eighth-grade graduating class.

Several events caused major changes in Alice's life at that time. Her grandparents moved out west to live with one of Alice's aunts, and her parents moved from the city to a suburban community. The family took occupation of their new house just two days before Alice entered the local public high school, a sprawling building teeming with about two thousand students. Her first few days were traumatic. All the students, having come from one or another of the lower schools in the area, seemed to know many of the other kids in their grade; Alice knew no one. The bell system signaling the end of one class and the beginning of another was unfamiliar to her, and twice she ended up in the wrong room. She spoke to no one, and no one spoke to her.

Throughout her first year of high school, Alice withdrew from all interaction with her peers. Sometimes several days went by when she did not speak a word at school, to anyone, about anything. The more time passed without speaking, the more difficult she found it to initiate a conversation or respond to anyone's casual overture. She wouldn't use the girls' bathroom during the day for fear of encountering another kid there. She joined no after-school clubs and made no friends.

Her increasingly concerned parents worried that Alice was becoming depressed.

The children I've described experienced a level of extreme distress. They all got better. Much better. They overcame their problems, with their parents' attentive support, by practicing simple skills that enabled them to bring their fears down to a manageable level. That, in turn, made it possible for them to engage with their worlds in a more appropriate way. They were happier, more full of fun, and more hopeful.

About Labels: A Final Word

We modern-day parents have gathered, perhaps been bombarded with, information from the popular media about all the dangers that can lie in wait for children, dangers our own parents probably never considered—the safety of childhood vaccines, autism, anorexia and bulimia, cyberbullying, academic pressures. We worry.

It's a small hop, then, to fret about the child who will eat only chicken nuggets or who needs a night-light. Or the child who refuses to go to a birthday party. Is that normal? Does he or she have a disorder?

Now that I have described these prevalent anxiety disorders and given them labels, I want to end this chapter with another message: don't worry too much about the labels.

Labels can help professionals communicate with one another about the constellation of symptoms a child is experiencing. Traditionally, the field of treating anxiety has followed a categorical model, placing a child in one neat category or another. That model attempts to reach consensus among clinicians about such measurements as how many criteria are needed and how long symptoms have lasted, in order to come up with a diagnosis of anxiety disorder. But in truth, children are different and families are varied.

You may have come to that conclusion yourself in reading over the "normal" and "not" parameters I've outlined. You may be saying, *Well, my kid sounds a little like this and a little like that, and I wouldn't say he's all that fearful all the time*... and so on.

The latest thinking in our field, and the basis of the suggestions in *Growing Up Brave*, is that the label is useful only if it leads us to the right treatment. State-of-the-art cognitive behavioral techniques are similar no matter which diagnosis a child receives. For all kids with anxiety disorders, we examine thoughts, feelings, and behaviors in terms of whether they promote or hinder a child's progress. We can't always capture a child's problems with the categories we have. In fact, we sometimes refer to "Anxiety NOS," Not Otherwise Specified, which is a kind of catchall term: something seems off, it doesn't fit neatly into one of our categories, but this child can benefit from our support.

Underlying all childhood excessive fearfulness is difficulty handling negative emotion, and highlighting symptom dimensions is a useful way of zeroing in on what a particular child needs. Shyness, for example, is usually a characteristic of temperament or personality, and not a problem unless at some point it interferes with what the child should be doing. Then we can teach this youngster some strategies—emotional tools—that will enable him to become a little more outgoing, have a little more confidence in himself.

My message to you is: the label doesn't matter so much. What matters is to recognize when your child could use some help. When you understand how anxiety works, and can accurately identify it as the source of your child's "acting out" or other issues, you can promote brave behavior and confidence at any age and in any situation. Know that there are core skills that can be helpful in treating all expressions of anxiety. And know that you can make a difference. If family history can't be changed, how you react to your child's stress-related behavior—your parenting style, we might call it—can profoundly influence his level of anxiety.

CHAPTER 3

The Attentive Parent

*How Parent-Child Interaction Styles
Affect Anxiety*

Picture this scene, a common situation that might sound similar to one you have encountered with your child at some point in time:

Charlotte, age 6, was embarking on the opening day of first grade. She was wearing new sneakers and her new Hello Kitty backpack. She would be taking the school bus to the elementary school about a mile away. Charlotte was apprehensive about everything—first grade in general, going to a school building that she hadn't been in before, riding the bus. As she and her mom waited at the pickup corner with several other parents and children, she was becoming unhappier by the minute.

When the bus pulled up, Charlotte got on, with a mournful look back at her mother. The following morning was worse. Charlotte was in tears before leaving the house. By the time they reached the corner, she was clinging to her mom, burying her face, saying the bus was going to make her get sick.

If that was you and your child, what would your reaction be? Here are some likely possibilities:

• You would reassure your child that everything was all right, don't cry, no need to worry.

• You would tell her, before walking out the door in the morning, exactly what she could expect throughout the day to come and how she would handle all that.

• You'd tell her to tough it out, get on the bus, everybody goes to school, everybody gets through it, and so will she.

• You'd promise her a treat in the afternoon if she stopped crying now and went off with the other kids.

• You'd take her home before the bus arrived, thinking you'd get her to school later on in some way, once she calmed down.

• You'd let her stay home.

• You would ask her what ideas she had to make things easier for herself.

No one of these responses is inherently right or wrong, good or bad. How you act in the moment will depend in part on the details of the day, the child, what happened the week before, what's going to happen next month, who else is on the scene, and other variables. But it will also have something to do with your style as a parent, the way you typically respond in trying moments. And we know that a parent's actions and reactions over time to a child's displays of fearfulness can either foster greater anxiety or reduce it.

In this chapter, we will look at how the characteristics of anxious kids and their parents interweave, and at how being aware of and making some adjustments to less helpful parental styles can change life for the better. At the same time, I want to reiterate a message I suggested in the previous chapter: Parents are not to blame for all their children's problems! Your child didn't "catch" an anxiety disorder simply from the genes you passed on to him. Neither did he become anxious because of everything that you've done wrong. Many influences in life can make kids anxious. You can't control it all, but there is a lot you can do to help your child get back on track.

Striking the Best Balance

In magazine articles and books and other sources of advice, you may have come across these terms often used to describe parenting styles: "permissive," "authoritarian," and "authoritative." Styles one and two, according to many experts, are less than ideal for the children living under them.

Permissive "anything goes" mothers and fathers fail to provide a child with any boundaries at all. Authoritarian "you'll do it my way" mothers and fathers tend to be emotionally withholding and keep too tight a rein on their kids. Authoritative style is the desired median with the best outcome: parents who both warmly respect a child's thoughts, feelings, and wishes, and establish necessary parameters, help him feel secure while promoting self-efficacy.

In developing the treatment of childhood anxiety disorders, we often refer to this goal as "attentive parenting": mom and dad are sensitive to a child's temperamental inclinations, and they adjust their protective and encouraging responses accordingly. We've also considered styles that seem to be associated with higher levels of anxiety in kids. We ask: In the parenting role, what is the optimal level of involvement? How much involvement is good and necessary, and how much is too much? And what does "too much" look like?

One more consideration: Does mom's or dad's personality

influence a child's responses to the world at large? Does a parent's behavior inform a child what's appropriate?

Current research points to two areas in which parents can inadvertently but adversely affect children's coping skills: by "overparenting," or being too controlling in one way or another, and by modeling anxious behaviors themselves. Some studies have suggested that anxiety in children is also heightened by highly critical, faultfinding parenting. In my observations over the years, I have at times seen a parent criticizing a child, but mainly I have watched the parent struggle to let go, to allow her youngster to make decisions and take actions, and to have confidence that he'll come out intact on the other end.

The "not letting go" is understandable. Meeting your child's needs for security and comfort, being totally involved in his life, seemed natural when he was an infant. You knew which cries meant he was hungry, or tired, or needed a diaper change. A crisis could be solved with a kiss, a cuddle, or a nap. Suddenly, and almost before you know it, he's more independent. His emotional and developmental needs are increasingly complex. You took care of everything when he was a baby. How can you best take care of him now? How does your role change and how do you adjust to those changes?

The challenge—and it is a tough one—is to recognize the difference between being an attentive parent and being a too vigilant, "too much" parent. It's balancing several powerful emotions: your fervent wish that your child have fun and make friends and enjoy being a kid, your protective instinct to ease his fears and take away his worries, and your desire to see him succeed.

The following scenarios demonstrate how these "too much" parenting styles play out. In each, the child, by nature or experience, tended to fall on the far side of the "what's normal, what's not" continuum of fears and anxieties. The parent was trying to do his or her best.

Controlling

The Too Talkative Parent

Offering a worried and anxious child a lot of information, or continually revisiting stressful situations in conversation, can fuel, rather than calm, anxiety. The kind of mental overload it produces often leads to what psychologists call "rumination" on the child's part—a type of thinking that can turn into persistent worrying or brooding. In addition, and most upsettingly, persistent worrying is sometimes linked over time to major depression.

The following illustrates one form of a "let's talk it all out" approach. It can be overdone. It can backfire.

An 8-year-old boy, Thomas, who was generally wary of animals, happened to see part of a nature show on TV that his older brother and a friend were watching. The show explained that pythons were occupying large sections of the Everglades in Florida, with some damaging results. A sixteen-foot-long python was displayed. The narrator described how pythons attack their prey and said they could attack a human.

Thomas was hugely upset by the images and the story. When he was having trouble going to bed at night, his mom questioned him about it and he reluctantly told her he was afraid to go to sleep because he might dream about one of those snakes. He developed a routine involving the arrangement of his toy action figures. He put them in a shoe box and placed the box under his bed before leaving for school. In the evening, he retrieved the box and lined the figures up in particular patterns around his room. One night his mother moved a couple of the figures to put a book back on the shelf. In the morning, Thomas became extremely agitated when he saw them in another spot. His mom thought he was acting strangely.

Thomas's no-nonsense parents, hoping to make him quit all the worrying, sat him down at the kitchen table and said, "Let's discuss this python business." They asked him what exactly was bothering him about pythons. Was it the way they moved? Was it because the creature was so big? Did Thomas's brother and friend like the nature show? Did he want to watch it again so it wouldn't bother him? Thomas didn't reply much to any of this. He didn't feel better either.

Another parent described her efforts to prepare her daughter for a summer day camp. Seven-year-old Ali's mom and dad signed her up for what Ali's mother called "a sweet, cheery, little outdoor camp that she'd go to on the bus for four hours a day. Two kids she knew would be there. No big deal. But true to form, Ali was worrying about doing this. She wasn't sure she would like it."

Her parents thought that visiting the camp ahead of time would make it easier. They arranged a private tour with the camp director, "a little preview, so she could see what it was like." The director met Ali and her parents at the front gate and walked them through the area. "He was lovely and inviting. He showed us the different tents for lunch and gymnastics and other activities. There was a swimming pool. We went down to a section that was a kind of miniature farm, with some chickens and a goat. The kids would be able to feed the animals, and if they wanted to they could take part in growing tomatoes."

Mom and dad were delighted. Ali, on the other hand, became more distressed as their tour went on. By the end of it, "She looked like she was going to cry. She wanted to leave," said her mother. The preview that was intended to relieve her worries only made her more anxious. So her parents thought it would help to have Ali watch an informational DVD about the camp. Over the couple of weeks before camp started, every evening Ali and her mom watched the disc showing kids frolicking in the pool, doing simple gymnastics, and singing songs.

All this seemed to weigh even more heavily on the girl. She brought up all kinds of problems. Would she have to feed the goat an apple, like the director had done? Because it might bite her hand. She didn't want to go in the pool. Suppose she didn't like the lunch.

Both Ali and Thomas were overwhelmed by their worry thoughts. Changing unrealistic thoughts to realistic ones is one way a parent can help a youngster get free of them (is it likely that a python will be on the loose here in the city? could you tell the camp counselor that you don't want to feed the goat?), and that's the subject of chapter 7. But it's necessary to fine-tune these attempts. If it seems that the child isn't benefiting from a lot of talking about the situation, and actually looks more upset about it, it's probably better to tone things down.

In checking out the summer camp, in person and on repeated video viewings, Ali's parents were trying to send their daughter a message: "We're going to look at it now so you won't be so nervous when you get there." But Ali might have been the type of child, as some are, not to want to test the water first; perhaps just jumping in works better for her. Having too much information up front exposes some kids to a greater degree of anticipatory anxiety.

The Intrusive Parent

When your child was a toddler, you got him dressed, tied his shoes, and cut up his food. At a certain point, you let him start struggling with these necessary activities on his own, in order to learn. Some research studies on parenting styles have involved videotaping parent-child interactions as the youngster is faced with a frustrating or challenging task—buckling a belt, for example, working at a shapes puzzle, or engaging in an emotional discussion. The investigators are interested in observing how much mom or dad steps in or becomes involved in doing the task for him. What these studies have noted is that parents of anxious children tend to be more intrusive and take over more than parents of nonclinical children.[3, 4]

Nolan was a bright and social 8-year-old with an impish grin. His mother brought him to see me because she and her husband had become concerned about his anxiety-driven perfectionism as well as separation anxiety. In second grade, Nolan had simply stopped participating, declaring that nothing he did was "any good" or "right." He'd begin a project only to rip it up. His teacher was pressuring his parents to have Nolan tested for ADHD. The boy was becoming disruptive in the classroom, purposely behaving in ways that caused the teacher to discipline him by telling him to "sit out" during certain activities; this was his way of avoiding those that he didn't feel he could do well enough.

In our clinic, I watched behind a one-way observation mirror as Nolan and his mom played in the room next door. Nolan took a container of red Legos from a shelf, carried them over to the table where his mom was sitting, and began to rapidly assemble them into small figures made up of just two or three pieces each. As he arranged them in several straight lines, his mother made an effort to engage him. "So what are these?" she asked. Nolan explained that they were his "monster bug army" and they were preparing to invade.

Picking up one of the creatures, his mother tried to become involved. "If they're bugs, should we make them have wings or something? Why don't you use some of these other pieces and stick them on like this?"

"That's not right," Nolan said. "They're not supposed to be like that."

"They're fine, Nolan," his mom said. "Why don't you make some more? I'll get some different Legos." When she returned to the table with several other bins with different-colored pieces, Nolan had already started taking apart the red creatures he had built. "These look dumb," he said. "They don't look like they do on the box. It's a stupid idea." He sat back in his chair, his arms crossed.

His mom persisted: "Now, honey, we don't say things are 'stupid.' And your monster bugs are terrific. Don't they look cool with yellow and blue?" She stuck some Lego pieces on one of the remaining red bugs. "Why don't you try making some blue or green bugs, okay?" She slid the box of blue Legos across the table toward her son.

Nolan knocked it to the floor. He jumped to his feet, his face flushing, as he screamed: "Legos are stupid! I'm stupid! I can't do anything right. I can't even build a bug the way it looks on the box! I want to leave." He ran over to the door.

In his mother's face I could read irritation, embarrassment, and a good amount of worried dismay. As a mom, I could understand her unhappiness at seeing her child fall apart over a seemingly insignificant exercise.

The Overly Reassuring Parent

In our research and observations of parent-child interactions, we see that the parent—often anxious herself—tends to be overly reassuring. This is a form of attempted control over a child's emotions. In a separation scenario, for example, mom says,

"Don't worry, you're going to be fine, you're going to love this," and so on. After enough of this kind of reassurance, the child is now doubting herself. She somehow hears through all the talk: *Hey, maybe Mom is actually worried about this. I'm not going to make it. Why is she telling me all the time I'll be fine? How does she know? Is there some reason I won't be fine?*

Nine-year-old Julia was nervous about attending the sleepover birthday parties that were common among her fourth-grade classmates. Julia's mom was aware of her daughter's nervousness.

On the way to one party, Julia's mother told her everything she'd packed in her overnight bag, reassuring her that she hadn't forgotten anything. They went down the list of items — pj's, robe, toothbrush, hand lotion. She reminded Julia that she knew the parents of the birthday girl, and of course Julia could call at any time during the party and she or her father would come to pick her up. "You'll be okay," her mom said repeatedly. "You'll have so much fun. I'm going to drop you off. Then what's going to happen is, I'm going to Dunkin' Donuts. I'll go for ten minutes, then I'll come back and just pop my head in and see how you're doing. Do you think that would be good?"

The more her mother sought to reassure her, the more stressed Julia became. Before they arrived at the birthday girl's house, she told her mother she really didn't want to stay for a sleepover.

Mom offered more reassurances: she'd talk to the other parent and let her know that Julia was nervous; she'd wait outside in the car instead of going for coffee. By the time they arrived, Julia was a wreck. Just as she had promised, her mother walked her into the house and told the birthday girl's parent that Julia had a hard time with sleepovers and might need extra attention.

The moment her mom left, the girl lost what little confidence she had. She wouldn't join the other kids in painting pottery and ran out to the car. "I don't want to go home. I just want you to stay with me for a little while more," she begged tearfully. Her mom, seeing how upset her daughter was at the thought of missing the party, agreed that she'd come back in and stay until Julia felt comfortable.

She never did feel comfortable. By the end of the evening, as the other guests ran off to change into their pajamas, Julia and her mother left. Julia felt she had "failed" again to fit in with her classmates; her mom wondered why her daughter couldn't just enjoy herself. But by offering her presence as a security blanket, she made it easy for Julia to avoid confronting her fears about spending the night away from home.

Instead of all those reassurances in the car, this parent might have changed the conversation to focus on what her daughter was most excited about or how proud she would be when she successfully spent the night at her friend's house. Predicting success for a child often creates it. Or this mom might have suggested that Julia would conquer parts of the evening and be rewarded, perhaps with a special mother-daughter afternoon at the mall, for toughing it out — a strategy I describe in chapter 10, "The Bravery Ladder."

Conveying an expectation of success isn't saying "You're going to be fine" fifty times. Instead, the message should be: "You know what to do if you need a little help, so now just go and have fun."

Modeling

The Anxious Parent

A number of recent studies on parenting anxious children have explored the issue of what is called "experiential avoidance," or, essentially, the tendency to avoid negative internal experiences or emotions. The natural instinct of a mother or father with low distress tolerance might be to remove the child from all anxiety-provoking situations or from the prospect of failure, as Nolan's mother was trying to do by finishing his task for him. By taking care of stress in their child, parents can avoid their own stress and make themselves feel calmer.

We parents have feelings, too! It is painful to watch your youngster having trouble. It can stir up the protective momma bear who'll do anything to make life easier for her unhappy child and take away the hurt. I've experienced the tendency myself when my preschooler was so hesitant and fearful about taking part in a dance class. I wanted her to enjoy the class; I didn't want to push too hard; I felt like relieving her of the pressure—all at the same time.

It's natural and adaptive to help your child when she is distressed, part of being an attentive parent. But letting her experience new challenges or work through her difficult emotions is also being attentive. Anxious parents tend to control more, and too much controlling results in higher levels of anxiety in children.

One critical parenting skill, then, is to learn how to deal with our own distress. Recognize that by encouraging your resistant child to enter a new situation, you're undoubtedly going to feel some tension, too. It might even be harder on you than it is on her. Remind yourself that you're helping her develop necessary resources by not always jumping in. Take a step back. Just watch. And often, when you take a step back, your child will take a step forward.

But another question: How do you handle stress in your life, aside from interactions with your child? We know that modeling behavior is one way we transmit fears and anxiety to our children, who of course are observing us all the time, not necessarily copying everything we do, but picking up impressions about how to approach the demands of the world.

The parent who described herself as "a nervous Nellie" and

who wondered if her son had inherited her anxious genes started paying attention to how she coped with everyday, run-of-the-mill situations that were on the stressful side. She observed, she said, "that I'm always running around like a crazy person. I never expect to be prepared for what's coming up. I make endless lists. If I buy something, I'm sure I bought the wrong thing. A lot of second-guessing. And my kids have often heard me talking about how stressed out I am."

She would never be "a relaxed type," she said, but she thought she might try to get better at living a little more in the moment. She was planning a short family vacation, a driving trip to visit Sturbridge Village and the Baseball Hall of Fame. "I decided I wouldn't line up every hotel or motel or restaurant. I told the family we weren't going to know exactly what might happen, let's just go and see where we end up. Have an adventure."

This was a big step for "nervous Nellie." It turned out well. Everyone had fun. And she was modeling for her child the sense that sometimes spontaneity is okay.

The Depressed Parent

Anxious parenting can present difficulties for children. But in being overly involved, doing a lot of talking, a lot of reassuring, mom or dad is at least attentive, all present. Depressed parents, especially mothers, typically are unable to engage with the child or care for him in the ways that are needed to ensure a warm parent-child attachment, and that can lead to significant psychopathology in kids, including depression.

According to recent studies, depression in children—the youngster takes no pleasure in toys, is irritable, doesn't want to play, seems sad across situations—can surface as early as ages two and three. In later years, he's often the "good" kid in school, quiet and tending to be timid and withdrawn, avoidant of engagement.

We're now seeing, in fact, that depression and anxiety aren't so different. Children depressed as preschoolers are four times more likely to experience anxiety disorder at school age. All this emphasizes the role of the parent in a child's development, and how important it is for any parent suffering from depression to seek help.

The Short-Fused Parent

Frank wanted to take his 6-year-old son, Jake, to get-togethers in their neighborhood park, where two or three other dads and their sons usually met on Saturday mornings to throw a ball around and play an informal game. Frank described his son as "like his mother, doesn't like to try new things." Dad himself was a gregarious, friendly man, a "big" personality, quite different from quiet, watchful Jake.

The first two Saturday outings did not go well. Jake sat on the sidelines and looked glum. On the third Saturday, Frank was getting testy. He felt, he said later, that he'd been encouraging during the previous weekends. Now he yelled at Jake to "grab a mitt, get out there, and run around, what's the matter with you?" Jake refused and started to cry, and said he was going home. Dad said, "You can't go by yourself. We'll leave when I say we're leaving." Jake picked up the bag with their things in it, dumped everything on the ground, threw the bag in the bushes, and ran off. His dad charged after him, grabbed him by the arm, and father and son left the park with bad feelings.

Another parent, the mother of a 9-year-old, described to me the efforts she'd made to engage her daughter in various afterschool activities. "Laura was always worrying that the other kids wouldn't talk to her," this mother said, "that she wouldn't be able to find a partner. Whatever the thing was." To persuade the girl to join a children's chorus in the community, Mom promised to buy her a special T-shirt she wanted. That worked, sort of, one time. Soon Laura was again digging in her heels. Mom said, "Please go, you'll have fun, we'll go shopping later. Maybe we can get that jacket you want." They did.

The following week, Laura said, "I'm not doing it. You can't make me." Her mother at this point was wondering if she was a bad parent. She was also feeling fed up. "I was giving her bribes to do this nice thing, which also happened to be an expensive thing. So I just said, 'Forget it. I'm not doing this again. This is a waste of my time and my money.'" Harsh words were exchanged. Laura said she hated her mom. Her mom said, "Fine, I'm not too crazy about you right now either."

There's a lot we bring to the matter of being a parent, all influenced by our history, our temperament, the ways in which we ourselves were parented. Parents who tend to have an explosive style, quick to anger, almost always regret the outbursts that seem to linger in the atmosphere. Even if there's no lasting harm done, children will more successfully develop their own coping resources when parents get control over their emotional responses. In fact, the occasional outburst, when a really aversive parent-child interaction develops—crying, hitting, harsh words—is often the signal that pulls a parent up short, and makes him or her think, *Maybe I need to change my style a little here. This isn't so good.*

It's hopeful and encouraging to remember that the dynamic between you and your child is constantly changing. There's always time to make it better.

When a Little Push Can Be a Good Thing

Here are two stories I've heard from two separate parents.

When Karen was 7 years old, her mother wanted the child to take part in some sports activities, or at least just one. Mom thought some kind of sports-related program would be a desirable thing, to give Karen an opportunity to "move her muscles," mom said, "learn how practicing and sticking with something makes you perform better. So we tried a bunch of things — karate lessons, swimming, modern dance. We tried gymnastics." None of this engaged Karen's interest. Initially resistant to start at all, she never warmed to any lessons and after one or two sessions, refused to continue. "She dropped out of every one of these," her mother said, "and it wasn't because they were too physically hard for her. She's a strong, healthy kid. I got tired of this routine. So one day I said, 'You know what, Karen? You're not going to choose to do *nothing*. You're going ice skating.'"

A small skating rink had opened up on the second floor of a building in their neighborhood, and a number of kids were taking lessons. Karen's mom signed her up. Karen protested; she wouldn't be able to do it; everybody else would be better. Her mom insisted, pleasantly, and took Karen to her lesson on most Saturdays. Karen never said she liked it much. After about a year, however, she had become reasonably proficient at several skating skills. At the year-end program for all the children, with parents watching, a videotape was made of Karen performing her routine to the soundtrack from *St. Elmo's Fire*. She was awarded a first-level patch to sew on her skate bag.

Her mother said: "She didn't stick with skating over the long haul. But recently I heard her playing that tape for a couple of her high school friends. And my now 16-year-old daughter says, 'I'm glad you made me do that, Mom.'"

Another parent, a summer camp story:

Twelve-year-old Zoe was scheduled to leave for a monthlong stay at sleepaway camp, one that had been thoughtfully chosen by her parents to be as minimally stressful as possible for their daughter. "Zoe continued to have a lot of separation anxiety around new things and places," her mother said. "This camp was not far away, low-key, not big on competition games or teams. Several of her school classmates would be going." But Zoe was apprehensive.

On the morning that Zoe and her duffel bag were to be picked up by the camp bus, the girl was nowhere to be found. The bus left without her. Her parents were not excessively worried and were pretty sure that Zoe was holing up in the public library, a couple of blocks away. There she was.

"Her dad said, That's it, and he went out and rented a car (we didn't have our own car), put the bag in the trunk, and told Zoe to get in, he was driving her to the camp. She was teary. It sounds like such a harsh, even mean thing to do, but you know, we were sure that once she got there she'd be absolutely fine. And she was fine." When mom and dad picked her up at the end of the four weeks, Zoe was a little teary again, this time because she didn't want to leave the fun camp and the new friends she'd made there.

Yes, attentive parenting means not being overly controlling, and taking a step back, and letting kids make their own decisions. But occasionally a child might need that extra push. Occasionally a parent, knowing her child, might be right to say, in effect, "Trust me, this will be a good thing, you will benefit from it, and that's why I'm deciding for you." Or saying, in effect, "Thinking about it makes it worse, and I know if you just go ahead and do it, you will feel very good about yourself, and that's why you're going to do it."

Children are resilient. They can learn hard lessons. But to grow up brave, they need the opportunity and psychological space to grapple with negative feelings and to navigate the sometimes uncomfortable but unavoidable experiences of life largely on their own terms. They need to experiment, need room to try things out. It's really about the development of coping resources. I think of it as emotional coping.

Earlier in this chapter, I described Nolan, the boy who flew into anxiety-driven tantrums when his Lego monster-bug army didn't look quite right. In observing Nolan and his mom at play in our clinic session, I noticed that like many anxious kids, he perceived his mother's questions and suggestions as criticisms. The more she asked him why he was doing something a particular way, the more he assumed she was telling him his way was wrong. This was similar to his behavior at school: the boy fell apart whenever accomplishments didn't meet his self-imposed expectations, and he withdrew from participating because of his fear of being found at fault.

In treatment, I helped Nolan learn to challenge his anxious thoughts and negative projections and worries, and replace them with a more positive and accurate outlook. In a few sessions — really, a short amount of time — he gained a great deal of self-control. At the same time, I coached Nolan's mom.

She began to recognize that by asking so many questions and making so many suggestions in her instinctive attempts to bolster her son's confidence, she was actually feeding his anxiety about not getting things "right." She learned the several important rules of "attentive parenting." She met with Nolan's teacher, and they discussed ways to help him engage in classroom activities with more confidence. All this had a wonderful outcome.

Nolan's mother followed up with me several months after I had seen the family, and she was thrilled to report that he was on track at school, with no more discussions of testing for ADHD. "I've got my sweet boy back," she told me. "He's stopped having tantrums and tearing up his schoolwork." What was just as gratifying to her: both she and her son looked forward to a special daily playtime, when he initiated activities he enjoyed and she practiced her new parenting skills.

Nolan was developing coping resources. So was his mother.

It started with a mere five minutes a day.

II

DAILY ROUTINES THAT WARD OFF ANXIETY

CHAPTER 4

Five-Minutes-a-Day Time

*A Simple Strategy to Set the Stage
for Brave Behavior*

When I work with the family of an anxious child, I first suggest to the parents ways to improve the secure attachment and warm connection between them and their child. I explain several specific skills to follow: "do" and "don't" rules. Then the child and one parent go into a room with some toys for a brief play session; as I observe, I offer suggestions—coaching—to mom or dad as warranted. The techniques are based on one component of a well-researched treatment called "Parent-Child Interaction Therapy" (PCIT), developed by Dr. Sheila Eyberg, a distinguished professor at the University of Florida, and her colleagues.[5,6]

What the parents at our center learn can be practiced—and should be practiced—at home.

You can think of it as playtime, positive play, or special time.

It takes five minutes a day.

A bit of background: PCIT is a type of intervention originally designed to treat young children with disruptive behavior disorders. Eyberg's program includes two phases—Child-Directed

Interaction (CDI) and Parent-Directed Interaction (PDI). They have been shown through numerous randomized controlled trials to be effective at improving both the behavior of children with oppositional defiant disorder and the general parent-child relationship.

Recently, these parenting strategies have demonstrated great promise with anxious children as well, helping prepare kids to begin increasing their brave behaviors and decreasing avoidant ones.[7] I will describe here how Child-Directed Interaction can easily be incorporated in your parenting "tool kit" for anxious children. In a nutshell, CDI involves you and your child spending a relaxed few minutes each day as you tune in to his state of mind and behaviors. You aim to enjoy your child and your time together. You let him lead the action while you describe and respond to what he's doing with approval and enthusiasm.

Here's why it's effective. Research has found that mothers and fathers tend to tailor their parenting to the kinds of children they have. An anxious child typically "pulls" reactions from his parent — hovering, correcting, excessive reassurances, disapproving looks — that are essentially unhelpful. Rather than encouraging growing confidence and independence, such responses tend to reinforce the child's sense that he can't handle things on his own. And he gets his parents' attention by being anxious.

During special time, which may feel and look and sound somewhat different from your typical daily interactions, you intentionally shift that dynamic. You allow your child to feel in control. You pay attention to positive behaviors. Practice five minutes a day according to the guidelines, and you'll begin to notice results. You'll find that the parenting skills you learn carry over into other parts of the day, with a beneficial influence on your child and on the overall atmosphere of your home. Your anxious child may seem calmer, more confident. His problem-solving skills may strengthen. As he moves out into the world, away from home base, he'll have a greater desire to explore new experiences and enter difficult situations.

Special time enhances your existing relationship. There's a little less tension and worry, a little more warmth and pleasure.

The Setup

Playtime is, as the word says, a time to play. It's easiest for parents to do with the youngest children, ages 2 to 5 or 6, but it still works with 6-, 7-, and 8-year-olds. With older kids, from roughly middle school age through adolescence, the five-minutes-a-day concept takes shape somewhat differently, as I'll explain later in the chapter.

Have a box or bin with toys that you'll use. Separate them out from the ones around the house, and tell your child that these are being set aside for a special time you'll have together. Appropriate items are blocks and other building toys, such as Legos and Tinkertoys; crayons and other materials for drawing and creating, such as clay and Play-Doh; things that both you and your child can do something with. Mr. Potato Head is usually a hit with young children. Dolls and play sets—farms, houses, and towns—are good. Pick out three or four toys your child likes for the "special playtime" bin.

One of the skills you'll practice is imitating what he's doing, and with building sets and coloring supplies, that's not so difficult. Avoid anything that might involve a competition, such as board games with rules and winning and losing outcomes. It's hard, obviously, when you're rolling the dice, moving three spaces, and keeping score to have the kind of relaxed, stress-free interaction you're after.

Avoid items like Wiffle balls or toy footballs, which can encourage play that turns too rough or wild. Avoid, also, superhero action figures; they often lead to pretend battle scenes. You don't want things to get too messy, so finger paints are not a good idea.

We usually don't include toy telephones and puppets. Puppets and telephones promote talking through something else, and a goal is for you and your child to talk directly to each other.

A 7- or 8-year-old might complain if toys seem too "babyish." Be sure to have age appropriate items; a marble maze construction game is one favorite with many somewhat older kids.

Set the five minutes, if possible, at the same time every day. Tell your child beforehand that special time together doesn't mean you're not going to play with him again later or tomorrow. At first, he might be a little suspicious about this attention: *Where is this coming from? We've never done this before.*

In our clinic sessions, I'll explain to a dubious child, "We're teaching mom and dad a special way to play. You might notice some differences." Mom or dad says: "I'm so excited to play with you and I think having a special playtime each day could be fun." This simple explanation should work at home.

Connecting with your young child in the way I'll describe can't really happen very well while you're cooking dinner and talking over your shoulder or driving in the car. Using the toys and joining children in their worlds is central to the technique. For five minutes, everything else stops. Get down on the floor or sit on the couch or at the table or wherever you're comfortable. Say: "You can choose anything you want for us to play with, and I'm excited to see what you're going to pick." Special time is under way.

The *Don't* Rules

I start with the "don't" rules, because these are usually most difficult for parents to abide by. After all, when mom asks her child a question, or offers suggestions, or instructs him to do something, she's acting, she knows, out of love and care and a wish that he succeed and have a good time. She's not angry or disapproving. She wants their five minutes to proceed nicely. So what's the problem?

All those well-intentioned intrusions on the activity have the effect of leading the interaction and lessening the child's control, and what anxious kids need most is to feel in greater control of their thoughts and feelings and behaviors. The "don't" rules encourage you to take a step back. Let your child be. Allow for silence. Follow what develops.

Here are the rules.

Don't ask questions. At all ages, this is a playful session. Nothing *has* to happen. Nothing *must* get done. Don't ask your child questions during these five minutes.

Of course, a natural question or two might come up, but I'm referring to the persistent questioning by which a parent, without meaning to, directs the activity or demands a response.

"Do you want to try something else now?"

"Should we use the Legos? You like the red ones, don't you?"

"Do you know what shape this is?"

Some questions are actually hidden commands.

"Would you like to clean up?"

"Wouldn't you like to sit over there?"

The tendency to pepper a child with a lot of questions is perhaps common to all parents. We want to know about our child's day, what happened, how she's feeling, what she's thinking. We want to instruct. I watched a mother and her child, a boy about 2, on the bus. Mom kept engaging him through a series of questions: "How many fingers am I holding up? How many now? Do you see that car out the window? What color is that? Is that the same color as our car?" and so on. Mom seemed determined not to pass up a teaching moment. The little boy went along with this for a while, answering politely, and then clearly had had enough of it. He threw back his head, twisted his body, and started to fret. He might have been saying, "Please stop this now. I just want to ride the bus in peace and quiet."

Kids can get turned off when parents are "at them" all the time. For anxious parents, concerned about their anxiety-prone children, stopping the questioning during playtime is the hardest rule to follow and the hardest skill to develop. Typically, the loving moms and dads in our clinic sessions have no idea that asking questions actually leads the play and subtly controls the interaction. When we start playtime, and after absorbing the rule, I often watch parents behind my one-way mirror begin to ask their child something, then bite their lip. One mother said just learning to cut out all the questions "was so insightful for me because I then had all this air space to say other things that were actually helpful and created a warmer feeling between us."

With practice, you'll get in the habit of rewording many questions to statements: for example, "Which one of the blocks do you want? What are you going to do?" can become "I'm excited to see which block you're going to choose" or "You always pick such cool colored blocks when you make a tower."

Don't criticize. A certain kind of criticism is common, seemingly benign, and difficult for a parent to recognize. It might not *sound* like criticism to say, for example:

"The horse should go in the barn over here."

"It'll work better if you hold your crayon this way."

"I bet you can stay in the lines if you try harder."

During special time, learn to refrain from making any such seemingly innocuous remarks. Remember that there is no *right* way of doing things. Your aim is to foster warmth and positive attachment, and to have fun together. Criticisms interfere with that process.

Don't give commands. When mom issues either an indirect command ("Let's put the cars away") or a direct command ("Come over here"), she is calling the shots.

The point of special time is that your child does the directing. He's in charge of what happens next. Don't tell him. Take a step back and allow him to lead the play. Follow his lead.

The *Do* Rules

The "do" rules follow the mnemonic PRIDE: *praise* appropriate behavior; *reflect* your child's talk; *imitate* her actions; *describe* what she's doing; express *enthusiasm*.

Do offer praise. Tell your child you like what you're seeing. Praise the process.

"Look how nicely you're drawing."

"You look like you're having so much fun making your picture."

"This was such a neat idea you had for building a castle."

"I really like how you're playing so carefully with your toys."

This is labeled praise, a positive reference to a specific action, choice, or accomplishment that you like. You're not calling your child the greatest artist in the universe. You're saying she's drawing carefully and you admire that. General praise—"You're a good kid"—is great for your child to hear, but if you "label it"—"I love the way you care for your brother"—that's even better.

Can this sound a little fake? I don't think so, not if you're genuine in your remarks and you talk in a manner that is familiar and comfortable to both of you. Saying "nice job on that tower" with a smile might feel more natural and more "you" than an effusive outburst with words you don't typically use. And something else it's helpful to know: Research has shown that for children with anxiety problems, and with behavior problems, you can't praise enough. They eat it up.

Do reflect what your child is saying. Your child says, "I drew a rainbow." You say, "You did, you drew a rainbow."

Child: "I like to make things with Play-Doh."

You: "You think Play-Doh is fun to make things with."

Do imitate what your child is doing. Your child tells you: "I'm putting all the cars on this side of the road." You say: "I'll put the trucks there, too."

She announces: "I'm changing my doll's clothes." You say: "I'm going to change my doll's clothes, too."

You may not even need to use words. He starts to build a tower; you gather some blocks and begin to make your own tower. It doesn't have to be exactly the same as his. What matters is that by imitating him, you are communicating "I like what you are doing so much that I want to do it, too."

Do describe what's happening. Describing is being a bit of a sportscaster.

"You're making a tower. You put on two more pieces."

"You drew a smiling face."

"You put all the horses inside the barn."

Reflecting, imitating, and describing might feel awkward, especially when you first practice the skills. Be flexible, be adaptable, and respond to the signals your child is sending. Obviously, you won't use these techniques constantly, with every tiny thing that arises. If she colors a big orange sun in her picture and sees you putting an orange sun in your picture and says, "Stop copying me," don't copy. Casually grab another piece of paper and say, "What you're doing looks like fun," and then draw a house or a boat. "We're drawing together. I like drawing with you." Leave it at that.

Interestingly, I have never seen young children really object to the praising, reflecting, imitating, and describing. Negative reactions have rarely occurred. Usually, in fact, I've been pleasantly surprised that kids go along with this so easily and willingly. It's probably a matter of *Wow, Mom is actually paying close attention to me.* That feels good.

Do express enthusiasm. You are there, in the moment, happy about being with your child and enjoying your time together. Show it.

None of this sounds like rocket science. You may even be thinking, *Well, I do all that already.* A parent who was skeptical about the process said, "This is just intuitive." But if you stick to the guidelines, you may begin to *hear* yourself differently. You will become more conscious of how you talk to your child during the day. You begin to recognize the kinds of responses on your part that contribute to a warmer attachment.

Here's a look at one parent and child who practiced special time in our clinic.

Five Minutes a Day in Action

Jeff and his 8-year-old son, Zack, had come in so I could observe how they were interacting. Zack's anxiety was beginning to manifest as separation anxiety with some features of obsessive-compulsive disorder, and Jeff, a high-powered architect, had called me to complain that although he had been setting aside the five minutes each day to spend special time with Zack, as we had discussed previously, he didn't think their relationship was improving. I knew he was skeptical that such a brief investment could yield significant results, and I wanted to see if he was following the simple but strict rules that govern CDI.

Father and son settled down alone in the play area. I watched from the next room through a one-way observation window; typically during these sessions, as at this one, I communicate with the parent through a "bug" in the parent's ear and a small microphone on my side, commenting on what's going on. I noticed that Jeff let Zack take the lead in deciding how they would play. That was good. The boy pulled out a box of wooden blocks and suggested they build a "superhigh tower." Jeff nodded and began setting up a base of blocks on the table.

"Let's move them to the floor," Zack said. "I want to make a tower bigger than me."

"Not going to work, buddy," his dad said. "You can't get a stable base on carpeting."

"It won't be big enough if we build on the table. I want to see if we can make it as tall as me," Zack protested.

"We've only got a few minutes and we want to build the best tower we can, right? And it won't be very good if it falls over because it's on the bumpy carpet, will it?" Jeff replied. "Don't worry, Zack, this will still be a big enough tower. Now, hand me some of those big rectangular blocks so we can get started."

Zack and his dad still had more than four minutes left, but already I could predict that before the session was over, Zack might have a meltdown—resort to his OCD ritual of having to tap each block seven times before placing it on the stack, or simply shut down. And that's what happened. After all, in the first thirty seconds of play, his dad had done all three things—issuing commands, asking questions, and criticizing—that I tell parents to avoid.

This father had the best intentions, but his style of interacting was actually reinforcing the boy's anxiety. Jeff instinctively wanted to help his child escape the upset feelings that came with failing at a simple task. His attempts to ensure a successful joint venture, however, led him to dominate the activity and inevitably resulted in a disappointing time for both of them. Jeff's behavior with his son was probably typical of a dozen other small interactions during the day at home.

You can see in this brief scenario both the simple structure of five-minutes-a-day and the not-so-simple effort that may be required on the part of mom or dad to stick to the rules. Being playful, letting the child lead, not taking over, is not as easy as it sounds. It may take practice. Jeff, in all probability, had some difficulty shifting from the demands of his work, living as we all do in today's stressed-out culture. In addition, he harbored nagging and persistent worries about his son's behavior. But we know that a parent's intrusiveness can be linked to a child's anxiety.

Over two more sessions, I encouraged him to take a step back, see what was going on, and interject remarks that might make the play more positive and more enjoyable for Zack. The more I praised dad for following the skills, the more he used them and the better at them he got. He began to realize how often what he said to his son could be heard as critical or disapproving. "Let me show you how to set that up" conveyed a silent message: "You're not doing it right." He learned to offer a compliment when something was going well or was nicely done. At the third session, the boy turned to his father at one point and said, "I really like building with you, Dad. Can we come back here and do this again?"

For Jeff, the light dawned. His initial reaction to the PRIDE skills had been: *Well, that's easy. I do that kind of thing all the time.* Now he said to me, "You know, it's not like we don't have these toys at home and we never play there. But I see it's not the toys or blocks. It's the way I'm connecting with my kid during the playtime that matters most."

This better connecting progressed. Dad learned to praise his son when the boy approached new situations, as well as when he resisted performing compulsive behaviors. Jeff noted big improvements in Zack's separation anxiety since they'd been having their five-minutes-a-day special time (and after we taught Zack some separate skills he could practice). When the boy participated in an activity that he'd previously avoided, such as going to a birthday party, his father remarked on it with a simple, "Good for you, Zack." Originally, the father didn't regard small steps forward as much of a success. His attitude had been "Okay, fine. We still have a long way to go, though" or "Okay, but it's like a needle in a haystack. That's just one piece of a big problem," and so on. Even his pats on the back were critical.

When father and son could find the humor in building a crazy structure that collapsed in a dramatic fashion, then the activity became pressure-free. Zack didn't feel the stress of needing to do something "the right way," and his dad didn't feel he needed to help him do everything "better." Several months after working with Zack and his father, they came into my office with photographs of all the crazy towers the two had built together.

Decreasing anxious behaviors, for any child, happens one step at a time, and each step is progress. A parent's role is to help her child realize he can take a step, and to build on it. Every youngster, like Zack, desperately needs his parent to be that affirming person.

Special time once a day is a start.

During the Preteen and Adolescent Years

The mother of a 13-year-old said: "When my son was younger, I was pretty sure I knew what was on his mind. Now I know nothing. And he seems to want it that way."

Her observation was partly accurate. We parents are pretty good at understanding what's going on with our youngsters. When they reach the preteen and teen years, they keep us more in the dark, but that doesn't mean that our children want us out of their lives and themselves out of our thoughts completely. A 13-year-old is trying to separate and individuate. With anxious, fearful kids, that process may be especially tentative or confusing. Teens who experience panic attacks and severe social phobias, which typically arise during these years, are usually keenly aware of how "odd" they feel and are reluctant to talk about thoughts and behaviors they can't help but find terribly embarrassing.

Anxiety disorders in adolescence not only cause misery for the teen but can disrupt family life in general. In chapter 11, I outline a course of action that works to reduce anxiety and associated problematic behaviors. And parents can absolutely be of help and support. In fact, some studies tell us that adolescents often make the most significant and lasting gains in treatment when parents are involved.

With kids from about age 9 through the teen years, we don't

formally call the process I've been describing Child-Directed Interaction, but you still have a vital role in sustaining a warm attachment. Obviously, the skills are applied a little more loosely and take a different tone.

You're not going to have a toy box. You're not going to build block towers. Imitating your child's behavior would probably go over like a lead balloon. Everyone likes to be applauded for what he's doing well, but at these ages children can become suspicious of praise they suspect is unwarranted or overblown. Certainly the "don't" rule about not asking a lot of questions holds true. Saying "Tell me about your day. What happened in school?" will cause many teens and preteens to clam up. At the same time, you *should* be aware of your child's day and how school is going. All the research shows that the more kids disclose—the more a parent knows who a child's friends are, what they like and dislike— the better outcomes they have in all areas, in school and peer social relationships, in how they do in life generally.

The trick is finding appropriate ways and times to interact, which may be just doing something together in a stress-free way, carving out that window of one-on-one time. It might be hard to arrange if your child is in a stage of blocking you out and only wanting to be with friends. But maybe say on a Sunday afternoon, "Want to go out for a walk?" "Let's go shopping." I've known anxious kids who love taking hikes with their parents, when the focus on a joint and vigorous activity—and not on them—is relaxing and welcome.

Step back. Listen. See what comes up, or what he has to say about his world. If nothing comes up, be okay with that.

Conversations in the car seem to be a rich avenue for connecting. Many older kids say they find it easier to talk when a parent is driving and therefore not looking at them; there's less pressure, less intensity. Reflect back the emotion your child is expressing, without passing judgment or offering advice. This can be especially difficult for anxious parents. It might take practice and heightened self-awareness to say, simply, "Wow, it sounds like that wasn't much fun." Or "You sound kind of nervous about the school play coming up." Or "I can tell you're excited about your birthday plans."

Show him that you're listening, so that he feels heard.

Why Five Minutes?

Research has shown that five minutes a day is sufficient for parents to practice the skills, and that having five minutes a day the child can count on strengthens the parent-child attachment and the child's feelings of self-confidence.

When PCIT was initially developed, researchers discovered that asking parents to set aside fifteen minutes or longer wasn't working. Parents were not compliant with the assignment because it was just too difficult to fit even that short span into a hectic home life. Before I became a mom, I tended to think, *Well, really, gosh, you can't find a few spare minutes?* Now that I have three children and a full-time job, and a need to prepare meals and generally keep a household running, I appreciate how tough it can be.

Five minutes is a span of time parents can commit to—and kids benefit from the predictability, consistency, and follow-through involved.

You are joining in your child's world 100 percent, fully engaged. And I can almost guarantee that she will come to love this period with you. You may start looking forward to it, too.

At the end of five minutes, of course you can keep going a while longer if everybody's in the mood and having fun and you're in the middle of a good, warm attachment; you don't have to call an abrupt halt: "That's it, time's up." You might say, "Okay, our special playtime is over now. I had fun! You can keep playing in the kitchen if you'd like while I start dinner. That way we can still talk." But don't put pressure on yourself and don't get into a half-hour session that sets you up for your child complaining the next time, "But, Mom, we did this more yesterday. I want to play more."

Tapering Off

How long should you keep up having special time on a regular basis?

As long as you like. Anything that can help your child feel she knows what to expect and therefore feel more in control of her life is all to the good. It doesn't have to be for the next ten years, but commit to this daily session while she's going through tough times. You can usually read your child. If you notice that things are simmering down, that she's making strides in overcoming her anxious behaviors, you may decide that three times a week is enough to sustain the positive interaction.

Nancy, the mother of 5-year-old Chrissy, had been frustrated over her youngster's refusal to participate in any kind of group activity with other kids. "Birthday parties, the Halloween party at our church, everything," Nancy said. "I wanted her to take this little ballet class, and Chrissy said she wanted to do that. We bought the ballet skirt, the shoes. We got there and, typically, she was pasted to my side. We got into our little push-and-pull routine, me saying, 'Go on, what are you worried about? Don't you want to learn to be a ballerina?' And Chrissy whining and saying, 'No.'"

That was when Nancy made the decision to take a step back, put the plans for ballet school on hold, and refrain from attempting to push her daughter into situations that she wasn't able to handle at least somewhat comfortably. She started the five-minutes-a-day time with her daughter. "That was really helpful for me," she said, "and an eye-opener. It took me awhile to get the hang of it, but we both, Chrissy and me, kind of settled down and relaxed more. I realized what was going on in some of these other areas, like the ballet. Even before we walked into the studio, I was all tensed up, anticipating that my kid was going to resist and be clingy and we were going to have another miserable, embarrassing scene."

Chrissy did get her mom's attention by the resistance and the clinging, but it wasn't a good kind of attention. The following autumn, Nancy took her daughter to the ballet school again. She watched as Chrissy quietly, shyly, walked toward the circle of other little girls. She turned back toward her mom, and Nancy said, "You know, I loved the way you did that." They both smiled. Chrissy was starting to separate.

Over time, parents begin to transfer special-time skills to the rest of life, making them part of their general repertoire. That's really the goal.

Two Parents, Two Playtimes

Should mom and dad both do playtime?

It's always best to have two parents onboard and acting consistently when helping a child overcome anxiety. Do try to set up two playtimes at home. Tell your child, "This is just you and me together, and later you're going to have special time with Daddy." Maybe she enjoys a different kind of play with dad than she does with mom, and that's fine.

When treating a family, we encourage both mother and

father to come in and have some practice with the skills. And sometimes the most dramatic and positive changes occur in the dynamic between a father and his child. These youngsters just blossom in the attention. In our research, we know less about father-child interactions because the mother is typically most involved. But I have observed many cases where kids, boys and girls, really long to spend this kind of time with their dads. If anything, it can feel even more special if they don't get to see dad that often in the course of a day.

When parents are divorced or in the process of separating, it's sometimes not possible for both to take part. Other times, one parent won't participate or sees no point or argues, "I'm not with my child very often. When we're together, I just want those to be good times. Fun times. I don't want to be thinking about a lot of rules."

The best outcomes take place when two parents are concerned about their attachment to their child and are able to say, in effect, "Okay, let's decide on one thing. Whatever else is going on, we agree on this, and that is that we each care about the well-being of our child. We want what is best for him."

Some truly heartening moments have occurred when parents, even when they are not on the best terms with each other, are able to appreciate and praise each other's interactions with their child.

One father watched with me behind the one-way mirror as his ex-wife played with their young daughter. At my suggestion, dad wrote down all the things she was doing well. We joined forces at the end of the session. I asked this father to comment on what he had observed, and he said to his child's mother: "Well, I thought it was great when you let Meredith pick out the toys. You looked like you were having a nice time. I could tell you were trying hard not to tell her what to do. Meredith seemed so happy." Meredith's mother was beaming.

Whatever else is part of the dynamic between two divorced or separating adults, appreciating each other as parents and saying out loud what's going right is only good for their child. And it can be good for the grown-ups, too. I've often heard from parents—and not only divorced ones—that their own relationship has improved, small positive shifts have taken place, because they've started to acknowledge each other as "a good mom" or "a good dad"—or, even better, have begun offering each other labeled praises ("I love how you get so into reading to the kids, doing all the different voices. You could be a professional actor!" or "Thanks for always remembering to put out the trash. I never have to worry about it").

The Challenges of Child-Directed Interaction

Many parents of anxiety-prone children are understandably anxious themselves. They're geared for the worst, "tensed up" as Chrissy's mother said. This matter of "taking a step back," allowing silence, giving the child some physical and psychological space, is tough.

When trying to follow the "do" rules, for example, they *over*do it. They hover. They have a hard time comfortably offering praise and reflecting back and so on. In our clinic sessions, the parent is sometimes so over the top that it's almost difficult to watch. One child picks up an airplane, and mom responds, "Wow! You got the airplane! Zoom, zoom! Here it comes! I just love airplanes!" She is certainly engaging, but too eager, constantly in his face. One child accidentally puts his hand by his crotch, and mom asks, "Oh, do you have to pee? I guess you have to pee. I really think you have to pee. Do you have to?" Finally the boy looks at his mother and says, "I don't have to pee!"

Some parents can't help praising an accomplishment without referencing a prior lack of accomplishment, which is something the child doesn't have to be reminded of: "You couldn't do that before, but now you can!"

Others make excessive use of "play talk," taking the "reflect back" and "imitate" rules to an extreme. They report feeling nervous about wanting to "play the right way," and that makes them talk in a kind of high-pitched, unnatural, nonstop manner. Their kids appear overwhelmed by all that persistent noise, and often just shut down and tune out.

These anxious parents want to do their best and engage in a supportive, fun way. But with such overbearing actions, they lose some of the genuine feeling of playtime. With further practice, however, they can reshape their behaviors into more appropriate, relaxed interactions. Indeed, parents have said they found it a relief to not have to "work so hard" at connecting with their youngster.

Another challenge comes up often with parents I meet, and it may be on your mind now. They don't see a need to get with the program. "What does CDI have to do with what's bothering my child, which is that she screams about school each morning and we can hardly get her out the door?" "My kid is terrified about going to sleep at night and we have to have lights on all over the place and sit in the room until he finally conks out. When are we going to talk about that?" Let's just skip this CDI business, in other words, and get right into helping my kid with his anxiety. Like many moms and dads, you may insist that you already enjoy a good, warm relationship with your son or daughter.

With the families I see, the child is the identified patient: get him into therapy, he has these problems, let's teach him how to get over them. But often what's hindering progress is transactional; it's what's going on between parent and child, the interaction, that needs to be fixed.

Which in no way suggests that you're a "bad" parent. Your general parenting skills may be excellent. But the special-time techniques will let you get away a little from the "presenting problem," and give you and your child a respite that does everyone some good. The mother of a 10-year-old girl with social anxiety said this:

"My daughter has always been shy. She always tended to have one friend at a time, which was itself a problem if that child decided to move on to someone else, like kids do. When kids in school started arranging themselves more in groups and cliques, Abby was out of it.

"I think I was more unhappy about this even than she was. She would walk home from school by herself, and if I'd call home from my office at three thirty and she was there, I'd feel upset. Crazy. You'd think I'd be glad that she was home safe and didn't get run over by a bus or something, but to me it meant that once again she didn't go to a classmate's after school to do homework or just hang out together.

"I was constantly landing on Abby about this situation — who was giving her a hard time, what this kid or that kid said, what else she could say or do, who she should invite over. I thought I was being supportive. Maybe I was just making things worse.

"We started with the five-minutes special time, which was actually longer than that, but I followed the rules. When I got home from work, we'd take the dog out for a walk together. I didn't ask her questions. Maybe she'd tell me about something she was reading or whatever. We usually ended up laughing a lot. It was a relief to me *not* to talk about her social life for a change. And she actually started having a better time of things at school."

It *is* a relief for a parent to switch gears a little. You're not always burrowing in on the issue that's bothering everybody. Kids feel bad about their problems. They know what's wrong, they focus on it, but often the constant attention ends up escalating or deepening whatever's amiss.

In our therapy sessions, we *do* talk about a child's separation anxiety or social phobia or OCD behavior. There *are* particular techniques—self-management skills or tools—that kids can learn to better manage their anxiety, and that is the subject of the following chapters. But interestingly, with the youngest children we often end up not having to teach the child skills at all. We see that after just coaching the parent, the kids start to improve. In one clinical trial testing the efficacy of PCIT for children with separation anxiety, once the parents practiced the skills and accepted the reality that some anxiety was normal and that they wouldn't be able to take it all away but could help encourage and reward brave behaviors, the children began to show significant improvements.

When There's More Than One Child at Home

Keeping up five-minutes-a-day might sound challenging if there are other children in the house. Special time has to be one-on-one. It's not impossible to involve two youngsters at once, but the warm connection, parent to child, is harder to achieve.

Can you wait until one sibling goes to sleep or is occupied with homework?

Can you carve out five minutes for playtime during the other child's nap or before she gets home from school or day care?

Or perhaps dad or another caregiver can take one child out for a walk while Mom plays with the other.

But when one child is struggling with anxiety issues and another is not, the whole family can be—and in fact usually is—unwittingly and unwillingly dragged into the drama. I've treated many families in which the parent says, *Our daughter is totally wrecking our home, she cries every night, nobody can get any sleep.* I've heard many kids describe the elaborate routines they have their parents going through in the early morning when leaving for school is so difficult.

One child can do soccer, the other can't separate to do soccer. So driving home after a game, while the parents praise the soccer player, how great she looked out there on the field, the other child sits silently, possibly angry at her sister for getting the attention. Or possibly feeling miserable and useless. Then mom and dad, who may have been bending over backward all week to accommodate her needs, become frustrated with her. She's exhausted their patience. There are no harsh words exchanged; the negative mood is not spelled out, but it's in the air.

Because a child's anxious behaviors can affect the peacefulness of the whole family, trying to create structure and balance is critical. Sometimes being overly involved with the anxious one isn't helping her anyway, while it's contributing to a tense and even hostile atmosphere in the home. In chapter 10, "The Bravery Ladder," I describe steps for the various anxiety disorders that are hugely successful not only in helping a child gain control over her fears but in restoring a little calm and reassuring routine in everyone's life.

If you are the parent of more than one, can you give each a daily special time?

What we observe is that parents who get good at CDI skills while interacting with an anxious son or daughter just naturally use them with the other child, not only during a set-aside playtime but in casual conversation throughout the day. They may start noticing positive effects, such as a boost in academic performance, though they never set out to "treat" this sibling. In fact, positive effects can be apparent in the littlest youngsters.

Some studies have indicated that "describing"—which I

referred to earlier as the sportscasting skill—helps 2-year-olds by improving or encouraging speech. I think you can start at an even younger age. At home, I use this skill with my 1-year-old during special time we'll have together while her two siblings are playing in a different room. For example, I might reflect back and describe what she's doing:

"Oh, you're picking up the blue book."

"I see you got your sock."

"You are taking such nice little bites of your cheese."

After consistent playtime with her, describing her behaviors and actions, she's now saying "sock" and "eese." I'm letting her know I see what she's up to and I like it. Just saying what she's doing makes for a richer play.

Praise is easy to offer and comes naturally. Expressing enthusiasm is easy, too, just letting your "other" child know you appreciate her accomplishments and enjoy your time together. None of this should be intrusive, getting too much in your child's face, filling the air constantly with words. Sometimes just sit back, watch, and listen. Allow her to have a little psychological room. Strike a balance.

Dealing with Misbehavior

In our work with young anxious kids, we don't see much defiance. Typically, the child is teary, tentative, or clingy. Yet there is sometimes an overlap between anxiety, especially separation anxiety, and misbehavior. Avoidance behaviors combine with disruptive behaviors, and it can be difficult to tell what's what.

The child is anxious and refuses to get ready for school. He throws himself on the floor, kicks, and soon has launched himself into a full-blown tantrum. Everybody's running late, tempers are short, voices are raised.

Another child won't leave for a birthday party; she says her stomach hurts and she doesn't feel well. Her parent tries to be encouraging and then cajoling, perhaps promising a treat later. The child still says no, and runs into her room and slams the door. Mom starts feeling upset with herself, wondering what she's doing wrong, and then feels angry. She shouts, "Okay, fine, stay home, then."

Sometimes the child is frustrated with himself for not being able to separate, and then furious at his parent for not helping him out. He cries, "Why can't you stay? I don't want to paint pottery with the other kids. I want you to stay next to me." Mom says, "I'll just be in the next room," but the child continues to protest, becoming noisy and demanding. It may look very similar to oppositional behavior.

The picture can be blurry. Is the behavior motivated by fear or by defiance? If your child is refusing to do something, is it because he's scared? Or is it because he knows that making a fuss is going to get mom's attention, push her buttons? *Maybe she'll start shouting or maybe she'll give in and not make me do the thing that's hard.* In both situations, matters can spiral down to a place where the interactions take on a negative tone. In fact, the parent is inadvertently encouraging misbehavior—by reacting to it with yelling and anger—or inadvertently encouraging avoidance.

If you begin five-minutes-a-day special time, the chances are your child will enjoy it and behave wonderfully well. But suppose he gets a little aggressive, pushy, and loudly insistent and directive? You can probably turn the tide by simply ignoring these attention-seeking outbursts and redirecting his focus on something quieter and better.

If what's going on can't be ignored—he's hitting and biting or throwing toys and chairs around—end the play. Tell your youngster, "We have to stop now because you hit me. You threw the train against the wall and it broke." Try to initiate CDI later in the day, if possible.

During play—or in fact, any time your child is refusing to go along with a necessary instruction—lead him in the right way. Try not to meet anger and frustration with your own anger and frustration. Don't let him push your buttons. Calmly remind him what he needs to do. Praise him at once when he does something right.

He learns, *This is what happens if I don't listen to Mom. Mom doesn't get bent out of shape, she doesn't yell at me, she just gently tells me what to do.* A calm response gives the child a sense of control. He knows what to expect if he does not comply with a parent's requests. The outcome is predictable, and he still feels respected.

Five Minutes a Day: The Payoff

The heart of Child-Directed Interaction—daily special time— is a technique that can be used with almost all kids. All parents can learn these basic skills; all children can benefit. While no research to date exists to indicate that this kind of therapy will actually *prevent* children from developing anxiety, we do know from our initial studies and clinical work that those with separation anxiety and other symptoms show significant improvement after treatment that includes CDI.

The key is consistency, predictability, and follow-through. In a world that can seem frightening and uncertain to your child, he feels better knowing that attention is coming from mom and dad at a regular, expected time every day. He knows he can count on it. During special time, he experiences control over part of his life. His sense of self-efficacy grows, the internal feeling that there are things he's good at, things he can do well.

Through CDI, you are setting the stage for bravery-directed interaction, the subject of chapter 10, which focuses on helping your child gradually begin to conquer his fears and successfully confront the situations that are hindering his progress.

CHAPTER 5

Managing Bedtime

The Benefits of a Consistent Sleep Pattern

Peter, a thin, dark-haired 9-year-old, was brought to the clinic because of an intense phobia: he worried that he and his family were in danger from intruders. In talking about his fears, it became clear that his anxiety over something terrible happening in the night was fed by images he glimpsed when his parents came home from work and flipped on the evening news. "There are lots of bad people in the world," he said. "I just feel safer when I'm next to Mom and Dad."

His parents, caught up in their son's nighttime anxiety, were allowing him to orchestrate the family's sleeping patterns. Here's what was happening. Peter refused to sleep in his room and wanted to sleep in his parents' bed. They didn't like that idea, but said he could stay on a mattress on the floor of their bedroom. If they tried moving their dozing son to his own room, he'd wake up screaming and crying. The commotion woke up his younger brother and sister, who would then also demand to be with mom and dad. Quickly picking up on their big brother's worries, they told their parents they were afraid to go back to bed.

Eventually, said Peter's mother, she and her husband had three mattresses spread around on their floor. The night was a moveable circus of groggy children rotating among beds, mattresses, and rooms. The parents were at their wits' end, not to mention half-dead with exhaustion.

Why is the matter of a good—or bad—night's sleep important in a book on helping children grow up brave? Increasingly, we are coming to appreciate the reciprocal relationship between sleep and anxiety. The more anxious a child gets, the more disturbed his sleep can be. The less satisfactory his sleep, the more anxious he becomes. The persistent inability to sleep well makes it harder for him to regulate his emotions and cope with stress during the day, and it shows in an impaired attention span, difficulties with learning, obsessive thinking, worry thoughts, impulsivity, and other troubles. Some studies have indicated that persistent sleep problems as early as age 3 or 4 are traced to anxiety in later years.

But the field of sleep medicine and childhood behavioral sleep interventions has traditionally been separate from that of child anxiety treatment. The approaches have developed in parallel, failing to inform each other. Research is just starting to show the wisdom of better integrating the two. And new research confirms what I've seen countless times in my clinical work with children and families: helping a kid get a better night's sleep, which doesn't take long, can have an amazing effect in immediately reducing the severity of his anxiety. And his parents are saying, "You know what? We're already feeling a lot better. He's not worrying so much."

The suggestions in this chapter concern good sleep habits and how to promote them in your home. They're part of a bigger message about the benefits of maintaining a reasonably predictable household routine. One team of researchers followed a fairly large group of children for thirteen years, starting from infancy, age one month. They found that when parents carried out necessary child-rearing tasks — feeding, putting down to sleep, diaper changing, comforting — at irregular times, with no consistent pattern of response, their babies grew up to display heightened symptoms of anxiety in middle school.

Children prone to anxiety especially find it reassuring when the basics of family life - -waking-up times, mealtimes, playtimes, homework times, bedtimes — can be counted on. They may not *know* it, but consistency in day-to-day activities makes them feel more secure and protected.

Along with five-minutes-a-day special time, establishing good sleep practices for your child can be a solid preventive measure to stop anxiety issues from coming up or from escalating. All kids really gain in confidence and self-control when they're well rested.

What Keeps Kids Awake at Night

Currently, I lead a team of researchers in the forefront of new and sometimes startling discoveries about the relationship between sleep problems and anxiety in anxious children. In a study of children ages 6 to 18 with diagnoses of generalized anxiety disorder, separation anxiety, social phobia, and obsessive-compulsive disorder, our findings pointed to a clear and strong association with sleep problems.[8] Ninety percent of these kids experienced at least one sleep-related challenge. Eighty-two percent had two or more, which included resistance or difficulty falling asleep, trouble staying asleep and then getting back to sleep again, and nightmares. For children with generalized anxiety disorder, going to bed often marked the beginning of overwhelmingly worrisome thoughts. Separation anxiety also tended to play out at nighttime, after a parent tucked the child in and left the room.

It's not just kids with diagnosed disorders who are caught in the fallout of unhealthy sleep patterns. For any child, poor sleep can exacerbate daytime stress, and, consequently, the stress parents experience. Pediatricians say that lack of sleep is among the most frequently mentioned complaints and reasons for parents to seek help. I recall one time recently when I took my youngest child, suffering from an ear infection and fever, to an emergency appointment with the fill-in pediatrician on a Saturday morning. The crowded waiting room full of unhappy-looking kids and their parents was not a place you wanted to be unless it was absolutely necessary. A woman sitting nearby holding a young child looked at me and said, "I'm here because he doesn't sleep, and I've had it. I want someone to give me an answer right now."

Her comment was an illustration of the degree of desperation parents feel when sleep is a problem—and of the desperation they express when they come for treatment of a child's anxious behavior in our clinic. Often in working with a parent, I'll start off by asking, "What's your nighttime routine like? How is your child sleeping?" Then we begin to explore how the family dynamics might be reshaped for a better outcome.

Behavioral insomnia of childhood, or difficulties initiating or maintaining sleep, has been tied to two areas of parental influence. One is inappropriate or inadequate limit setting, the failure or inability to stick to a fixed routine surrounding bedtime. In one household (this is a rather extreme example of a lack of limits), the mother, a hardworking corporate executive, came home at irregular hours worn out from her job, grabbed some leftover food from the refrigerator, and went into her room to rest, in essence posting a Do Not Disturb sign. The father fixed a quick dinner for the kids, then settled in front of his computer to correspond with his overseas clients. Their two children were left to their own devices to do homework and get to bed, some time or other.

The second area is related to sleep associations, the kinds of assistance a child comes to need—maybe lights, sounds, a parent lying in bed with her—in order to sleep. One child made repeated requests for water or blanket adjustments, getting her mother to return to her room half a dozen times or more. Then mom was to remain in the glider chair across the room until the girl fell asleep. If the child woke up in the night, she was unable to fall asleep again without water and blanket adjustments and mom in the chair, the cues she associated with bedtime.

The good news is that anxious behaviors improve when sleep habits improve. We've demonstrated clinically that when children receive a brief sleep treatment, just three sessions, and parents learn a few basic strategies for establishing positive family and bedtime routines, the children showed reduced nighttime fears—even without the anxious behaviors themselves being targeted for attention.

Learning the basics starts with an appreciation of what is called "sleep hygiene."

Sleep Hygiene

A number of factors affect how well a child sleeps. Consider the following guidelines as just that, guidelines, and see how they fit into your family life. It might be nice if every young child went to sleep at 8:00, 9:30 for the adolescents, but obviously that's not always going to happen. In trying to turn around frustrating evening and bedtime practices, come up with a plan that feels realistic.

The elements of sleep hygiene:

Bedtime consistency. Your child goes to sleep and wakes up at the same time each day, within thirty minutes. Even on weekends.

Even in the summer. That's the gold standard and probably not realistic, but the more a child can adhere to a regular schedule, the better his biological clock functions—the internal mechanism that controls sleep-wake cycles and that tells him it's normal to be awake when the sun is up and not when it's dark.

Bedtime environment. A child's bedroom should be an inviting and relaxing place, with—at nighttime—little noise and light and a comfortable temperature. It's an area that should promote sleep, in other words, and therefore at an agreed-upon hour TVs, computers, Xboxes, Wii's, cell phones, and other arousing items need to be turned off, disconnected, or removed from access.

Not so easy to accomplish, perhaps, if your child has become accustomed to all manner of activity in his room, all the time. With some kids who have trouble falling asleep, we try to encourage what we call stimulus control; the bed is a place associated with sleeping only. So the child is instructed to avoid hanging out there at other times during the day and evening reading, playing video games, doing homework, or talking on the phone. Bed = sleep.

Bright lights are undesirable because they function like the sun, causing the brain to continue in an activated state. Even if the child is dozing with a light on, sleep is not as sound and restful as it should be. Also, of course, needing a night-light can interfere with a child's social life. Sleepovers are difficult or impossible if a child can't go to sleep without it.

Bedtime ritual. If one is not already established, develop a soothing, pleasant bedtime ritual. For a young child, this might include a warm bath, getting into pj's, and a brief story time. Have three or four regular activities that signal "bedtime." They should last for about twenty or thirty minutes; don't extend it. Make it a little fun, just a comfortable way to close out the day—reading together for a while, some conversation. Don't talk too much about the following day, however, because that often starts worry thoughts. Don't talk too much about the day just past ("Was anybody mean to you in school today?"), because that opens a can of worms. Just relax.

For an hour before you start the bedtime routine, avoid any arousing, high-energy activities, like running around, shooting hoops outside in the yard, or playing video games. TV, ideally, is off.

One father began the habit of reading to his daughter for half an hour before her lights-out. She'd get in bed, and dad would lie on the guest bed in her room. He decided, he said, "to make this kind of interesting for myself. Not all Beatrix Potter stuff. I read some Shakespeare, *Much Ado About Nothing, All's Well That Ends Well*. A little Wilkie Collins, because I like him. I did do all the Nancy Drew books. Some of what I was reading was clearly over her head, but that didn't seem to matter. It was just a peaceful, quiet time. Probably the sound of my voice made her drowsy." Years later, his daughter remembered those peaceful, quiet times with great fondness.

Things to avoid. Daytime naps (almost all children no longer require morning or afternoon naps by ages 5 to 6), caffeinated food or drinks (including chocolate) within six hours of bedtime, large snacks or liquids within two hours of bedtime, and exercise within an hour of bedtime should be eliminated.

Relaxation exercises. Worry thoughts keep kids awake, even when they might desperately want to sleep. Relaxation exercises can be a calming and effective part of a positive bedtime routine, and there are several strategies proven to promote sleepiness. An exercise designed to release muscle tension throughout the body is described in chapter 8.

* * *

That's sleep hygiene. All well and good, you say, but how is it accomplished? You might start with monitoring. Set up a sticker chart on which you write down and keep track of the precise behaviors you want your child to exhibit in getting to bed. It's a strategy that works in turning around a nighttime routine that has disintegrated into chaos and frustration.

The Bedtime-Monitoring Checklist

Develop a bedtime list to monitor your child's appropriate behaviors. This is also where you will keep track of his successes, rewarding each with a gold star.

On a large piece of poster board, make a calendar. Going across horizontally, mark off columns for days of the week. Going down the left side vertically, mark off a space for the actions you want to see happen.

Choose several target behaviors to monitor. Tailor the checklist to fit your needs. All families are different. Some are more relaxed about the time for lights-out, some like an extended snuggle time. Include one behavior that you know your child can already accomplish. Maybe he's good at putting on his pajamas. That's a built-in success. Set up the list according to a specific routine, what you want to see first, second, and so on. You might want to draw pictures of what will be happening, especially encouraging for younger children. Kids often get a kick out of helping with the bedtime checklist poster.

Here are some common items (choose four or five, or create some of your own):

I brushed my teeth.
I took a bath.

I put on my pajamas without anyone having to remind me.
I went upstairs to my room.
Mom read a story, and I didn't ask for another one.
I said good night.
I didn't call out when I got into bed.
I read quietly in bed.
I went to sleep with the light off.
I stayed in bed until morning.

Place the checklist poster in an area of the house where every-one can easily see it, such as the family room or the kitchen, and fill it out consistently each day. In the morning, parent and child look at the chart and see how much he accomplished. The child gets a happy face or check next to each behavior he successfully completed. If he managed all of them, he gets a sticker in the calendar box for the previous day, when he had a brave night. After ten brave nights in a row, he might get a bigger reward, like a family pizza party.

Monitoring is a tremendously effective way of changing behavior. The child becomes more self-aware, knowing that a parent is keeping track of his progress and applauding his accomplishments. In fact, a series of studies have shown that this strategy produces rapid behavioral change, often within two to three weeks of consistent use.

Praise for the Smallest Steps

Anxiety over bedtime can be driven by internal triggers—worry thoughts, such as Peter's fear of intruders—or external triggers—too many lights, too much noise. Sometimes, however, what's going on isn't anxiety at all, but oppositional behavior. I commonly see this in families with a preschool or young school-aged child. He simply wants the day to keep going, and he'll stretch out the evening routine in any way he can.

It drives parents nuts. I hear so often that mom or dad gave in to the "just one more" request and joined the child in bed or on the couch to read a story, to settle him down; then mom or dad dozes off, child is still going strong, parents have lost their evening adult time. But even when a child is not motivated by fears, the fallout from a delayed bedtime is still harmful. Especially for one with a nervous temperament or one who is prone to anxiety, insufficient sleep has unwanted ramifications for his ability to cope with stress during the day.

One 6-year-old had perfected an elaborate, drawn-out nighttime routine. Michael was allowed to watch a TV show in the evening. As soon as it ended, the battle started. He wanted to watch one more. Sometimes his parents said, "Okay, just one more. You can watch as long as you don't cry and fuss when it's over." When it was over, Michael cried and fussed. Typically, then, his parents got fed up. "That's it! You do this every night! No more!" The next night, however, was a repeat scene.

When the TV was finally off once and for all, parents and child engaged in a series of negotiations about what came next. He'd insist that dad check that all the windows and doors were locked. Then there were fights about brushing his teeth. He didn't want to put on his pajamas. Michael had trouble transitioning from one activity to the next, with tantrums in between. Eventually, they'd get him upstairs, but the whole scenario was one long series of negative parent-child interactions, from the moment the word "bedtime" was spoken.

In our treatment, Michael's parents were encouraged to ignore the oppositional behavior and simply not respond to the tantrums. "But we do ignore his tantrums," they insisted. "We don't give in when he starts up all this noise about brushing his teeth and getting out of his clothes." They came to realize that just by watching their son's meltdown, with disgruntled frowns on their faces, arms folded in anger, they were actually responding to the negative behavior, keeping it alive.

In their march toward establishing better limits for Michael in the evening, this mother and father learned to pay less attention to his tantrums and matter-of-factly carried him upstairs to his bedroom. But first, we drew up a monitoring chart with pictures to illustrate every step of the routine. Mom laminated the chart depicting all the stages of "now it's time to get ready for bed." Each step he completed earned him a gold star sticker. If Michael started to have one of his blowups, she'd simply point to the chart and say, "Michael, what's the next step? I can't wait to give you a star." She ignored the negative and instead set up the expectation that the boy could do it.

And then mom and dad laid on the labeled praise.

A treatment strategy known as "shaping" works wonders in inching a child toward a desired outcome. Basically, shaping involves responding positively and immediately with praise to even the smallest step toward the behavior you want to see. Shaping is similar to the "Bravery Ladder" techniques I'll describe later, in chapter 10, but in this case, "inching" is the operative word—taking little baby steps in the right direction gets a lot of positive attention.

We use shaping with children who display selective mutism, refusing to speak to certain individuals. First, the child is encouraged to whisper softly into a tape recorder, and gets praised for that accomplishment. She speaks a little louder, and then a little louder still. Finally, she tries out her speaking skills with the designated person, all with a lot of immediate positive reinforcement.

Shaping worked well in turning things around for Michael

and his parents. If he made even one move toward the stairs, they'd say, "Oh, you're getting ready to go upstairs. Good for you." They used little games, making the routine kind of fun; one evening he'd hop over toward the stairs, or walk sideways. He began saying proudly, "I can do the next thing. You don't have to tell me," and they'd reply, "Oh my goodness, this is so terrific," and when he did complete a step on his chart without mom or dad having to remind him, he got a kiss, an instant reward for the good behavior, just a lot of great, juicy enthusiasm right away.

Very soon, Michael was getting to bed on time and enjoying a good night's sleep.

Countering Bad Bedtime Behaviors

The goal is to have your child eventually fall asleep on her own, in her bed, at the agreed-upon hour, and sleep there through the night. So the habit of staying with your child until she falls asleep, for example, or allowing her to crash in your room should slowly be eliminated. It's a process called "graduated extinction," based on the understanding that when inappropriate behaviors are largely ignored, they wither and die on their own over time.

Here are the rules.

• Ignore your child's protests as much as possible and stick to the routine you've established. If she's crying or yelling, calmly explain that it's bedtime. Don't engage in an argument or debate.

• Don't make "deals" with your child about staying up later. If after a lot of whining about "just another half an hour," you say "okay," you are reinforcing an inappropriate behavior and teaching her that you will allow, and even reward, this kind of thing.

• If she gets out of bed or leaves the room after the bedtime routine has been completed, firmly and calmly remind her that it's bedtime and send her back to her room. Ignore any continued protesting. A young child might need to be firmly and calmly carried back to her room.

- If she's calling out or crying but remaining in bed, simply remind her that it's bedtime. If the crying and calling out continue, you may want to develop a check-in schedule that is gradually phased out—for example, looking in on her once every five minutes, then every ten minutes, fifteen minutes, and so on.

All the same, I would never say never. Things come up. There are special celebratory nights. Sometimes a child is sick. But in general, try to stay close to the routine, and make it clear that everyone in the family must be on board. Everyone wants to feel better, rested, ready for the next day.

Sleep and the Resistant Adolescent

Developmental and physiological changes as a child grows older also change the look of sleep. Newborns, we know, typically sleep for fifteen to eighteen hours a day. Eventually, in later infancy, sleep is redistributed so the baby is taking a morning and afternoon nap. Three-year-olds are still taking one- or two-hour naps in the middle of the day. By ages 7 to 12, sleep usually decreases to ten or eleven hours a day, and for teens, the number is said to be slightly over nine hours. But many adolescents may need *more* sleep than they actually get, and due to natural shifts in their circadian rhythm, they often prefer to get it at odd hours, like the kid who's still in bed at noon on a Saturday. Adolescents, unlike younger children, tend to stay up later and sleep later, natural for this phase of development. In addition, as many as 45 percent of kids ages 11 to 17, according to some studies, actually get *less* than eight hours a night.

There's nothing wrong with a slightly fluctuating bedtime, but if a teen is regularly turning the lights out at 1:00 in the morning and must leave for school at 7:30, she'll pay the price. For parents, setting limits on teens, however, is notoriously difficult. The children I work with up to about age 10 are delighted with the sticker charts and earning small rewards. It doesn't work with adolescents. And many kids in these years are pursuing active social lives that continue into the night. Everyone stays up late. Over time, natural sleep rhythms may be seriously disrupted and sleeping—or not—becomes a troublesome issue.

Carly, at 14, was an accomplished gymnast, an A student, a girl with tons of friends. Despite her successes, she wasn't sleeping well. Her routine was going to school, rushing to gymnastics, coming home and getting on the computer, fighting with her brother a little, having dinner, starting homework. Then thoughts about her homework, getting it finished and getting it right, made her anxious. At our first interview, her mother said, "I have a high-functioning kid. Can you please help her sleep?" Mom was exhausted, the family was on edge; it became clear that nighttime-and-Carly was a huge topic of conversation and attention, every day. Even when they stayed over at a hotel during a trip, Carly would warn ahead of time, "You know, I'm not going to be able to sleep."

Her mother, fairly desperate, had tried anything that offered a promise of relief. She researched herbal remedies touted to improve sleep, and Carly took a variety of these, with no clear effect. Mom gave her melatonin pills, supplements based on a natural hormone the body produces when falling asleep; still no improvement. It was next to impossible for her parents to wake Carly in the morning without literally pushing her out of bed, and for a while her mom offered bribes. If Carly would just get to bed on time and wake up on time and do it for three days in a row, she'd get the new running shoes or sweater or whatever she had her eye on. This tactic sometimes had a short-term success, until it didn't. Here's where the picture got a little cloudy: Carly was perhaps a tad manipulative in the whole scenario. Was staying up late working for her, earning her a few desired treats or gifts from time to time?

At that first meeting, mom said, "This problem is affecting us all. I'm really done with it."

In working with Carly, the first challenge was persuading her that this not-sleeping issue was important. She didn't actually think it was a big problem for her, that it was more one for her mom. Through a strategy called "motivational interviewing," I encouraged her to come up with the reasons it might be in her benefit to get more rest, essentially a process of asking what *wasn't* working. And she was able to list a few difficulties once she gave it some thought.

She recognized that she was often tired, that some days she wasn't alert in gymnastics. Also: "I get cranky, I get into arguments with my family, and I don't really like to do that. For some reason, I think I'm going to fail at this sleep thing. It's really important for me to do well, and I'm afraid I won't be able to do this." That explanation was consistent with her perfectionistic personality.

Carly was staying up until midnight. "If I lie down at ten or earlier," she said, "there's no way I'll ever fall asleep. I'll just lie there worrying I won't be able to sleep." She was still doing homework or, usually, texting her friends while in bed. Like many teens, she was quite adept at it, texting in the dark with her cell phone under the covers, so mom didn't notice if she looked in. Chatting with her friends this way was relaxing, Carly insisted.

Her typical afternoon and evening didn't include much downtime. So we worked out a restructured plan for her evening, from the time she got home. She would start homework before dinner, all to be completed no later than 8:00. Carly agreed that this deadline was realistic. She also decided to move her shower from morning to evening.

We gradually shifted her bedtime a little earlier, in fifteen-minute increments. The eventual goal was lights-out at 10:00. If she was unable to fall asleep after fifteen or so minutes, she was to get up, turn on a light, and do some light reading. We didn't want her to be worrying and stewing about sleeplessness.

Mom would set a limit on texting. If Carly was done with homework and in bed, she could text up to 10:00 and then mom took the cell phone into her own room. Carly had often stated that texting her friends was a way she relaxed, but in fact, all that contact was keeping her brain on alert, thinking about peer dynamics, relationships, all the drama that goes on with 14-year-old girls. If she absolutely had to start texting, she agreed that she'd get out of bed and do it in another room. This activity was not to be associated with bed and bedtime.

She practiced muscle relaxation, which I discuss in chapter 8, to occupy her instead of lying in bed worrying about not sleeping.

Within three weeks Carly was falling asleep regularly. Three months later, she said she felt other areas of her life had improved. Her homework was finished earlier, she felt more rested during the day, and she found a couple of subjects she'd always struggled with were now easier.

She was feeling proud of herself. She'd accomplished the thing she'd believed was impossible.

Insomnia can take root with a teenager as a result of a combination of factors—anxiety over school or social life, doing homework into the night, a sleep-wake rhythm that is thrown off-kilter by episodes of crashing for twelve hours on weekends or holiday breaks. I've often worked with parents who felt helpless over how and when to insert themselves into the picture. "You can't tell these kids what to do," said one father. I think you can, however, open the conversation, appreciate the child's arguments about "everybody" staying up late, and negotiate some compromises around establishing a better bedtime. Often, even a resistant teen will acknowledge her need for more sleep.

At the beginning of this chapter, I related the story of Peter and his family, where matters had degenerated to the point of mattresses spread around the parents' bedroom every night. To turn the tide, we employed several of the strategies I've described, including shaping, taking tiny baby steps toward the hoped-for outcome. That meant moving Peter out of his parents' bedroom. His mom and dad gradually eased his mattress farther away from their bed, five inches at a time. Soon it was no longer in the room but in the hallway. They were getting somewhere.

His parents designed a bedtime behavior chart that displayed all the activities he was expected to manage, and Peter was rewarded with tokens redeemable for special treats when he completed the steps on his own. They created a stress-free environment, for their children and for themselves, by shutting off all TVs and video games in the bedroom. After a month of consistently following the plan, Peter's now well-rested parents called to say everyone in the family was sleeping soundly in their own rooms. In addition, Peter's teacher remarked on his improved performance in school. They made an additional improvement in the home; instead of flipping on the news after dinner, everyone relaxed by playing a board game. Peace had been restored.

Many parents I see start off saying that bedtime in their home is just, well, a nightmare. They dread all the pleading, all the whining, frayed tempers, parents and kids unhappy with one another. And this is night after night. The youngster who's fearful of dogs, after all, doesn't have to see a dog every day. But everyone must sleep.

After they've spent some time learning strategies to change a malfunctioning routine and all is running smoothly, these same mothers and fathers often report that bedtime is the best part of the day. They've taken back control of their household in the evening. What makes it work is consistency, predictability, and follow-through.

III

STRATEGIES TO LESSEN ANXIETY AND PROMOTE BRAVERY

CHAPTER 6

The Cycle of Anxiety

A Three-Component Model

Becca, a quiet 13-year-old being treated for panic disorder, was cataloguing her reactions as I walked with her down the steps into the Boston T station. We were conducting a controlled exposure to a situation—in this case, taking the subway—that triggered Becca's panic attacks, in order to help her understand their mechanics and learn that her anxiety would not hurt her and would naturally dissipate.

"Okay, my heart is beating really, really fast," she told me as we approached the ticket booth. "I'm shaky. I feel sick. Everyone is looking at me. They can tell something's wrong....I'm going to embarrass myself right here in front of everyone....I think I'm going to throw up....I've got to leave....My fingers are tingling....Something's wrong. My body is not normal, not like other people...."

Becca asked me for her cell phone. She wanted to call her mother because just hearing her voice usually made her feel better. When she called her mom at a stressful moment, she'd always ask the same thing: "I'm going to be fine, right? Everything is going to be fine, right?" And her mother had to reply in a particular way, with the same words every time, or her panic would escalate. Becca also carried with her several "safety" items—a water bottle, a piece of her old security blanket, and a note from her grandmother—that she patted for reassurance.

Becca was caught in the cycle of anxiety. Her worry thoughts (*if my panicky feelings start, what if they don't stop?*) provoked scary physical sensations (rapid heartbeat, nausea, tingling in her hands) that then drove her to specific coping behaviors (drinking water and calling her mother). The more she avoided going places, the bigger her worry thoughts grew, the stronger the sensations, and the more crucial her safety net. Her anxiety had reached the point at which it was ruling her life.

I was coaching Becca, urging her to describe what was going on in her mind and body and the behaviors she endured during a panic attack in the subway. But in fact, all children at times of heightened anxiety experience the same three-part event: a self-reinforcing combination of thoughts, physical sensations, and behaviors that can easily overwhelm them.

The Cycle of Anxiety

When I talk to parents at our treatment center, to explain how anxiety works, we begin with the diagram on the opposite page.

The top bubble is for the child's anxious thoughts, the images or possibilities that enter his mind when confronting a scary situation. He may or may not be entirely aware of his thoughts, the thoughts may not be factual or accurate, but they are causing deep distress. Some examples of anxious thinking:

"Something will happen to me when Mom leaves."
"What if my parents don't come home?"

"Maybe I'm dying."
"Maybe I'm going crazy."
"Everybody will think I'm stupid."

The bubble on the lower right is for the child's anxious feelings, the physical sensations that arise at stressful times. They can include a pounding heart, rapid breathing, sweaty palms, dizziness, stomachaches, tingling, shaking, headaches, hot or cold flashes, breathlessness. These alarm reactions are a natural function of anxiety, a response to fear or suspected danger, and won't hurt the child, though he probably doesn't realize that.

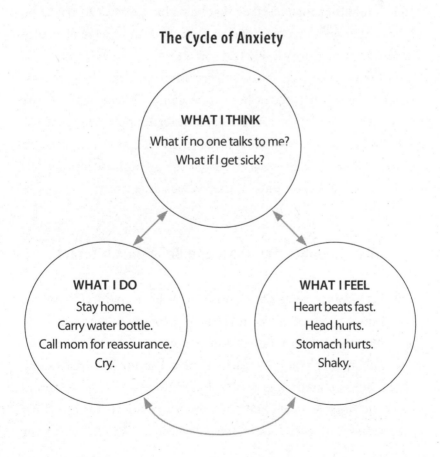

The Cycle of Anxiety

WHAT I THINK
What if no one talks to me?
What if I get sick?

WHAT I DO
Stay home.
Carry water bottle.
Call mom for reassurance.
Cry.

WHAT I FEEL
Heart beats fast.
Head hurts.
Stomach hurts.
Shaky.

The third bubble, "What I Do," encompasses unproductive, undesirable coping behaviors the child exhibits during threatening situations, which further reinforce the cycle. You are probably familiar with some of them: clinginess, crying, tantrums, complaints of feeling sick, avoidance of anxiety-provoking activities, carrying objects for "safety."

As you see, the arrows indicating movement or influence go in both directions. There is no one "start" point or "end" point.

Every child is unique. The cycle can begin with any element. For Becca, worry thoughts were the trigger.

For some children, anxiety is typically set in motion by a sensation in the body. Bobby, let's say, notices that his heartbeat seems louder and faster than usual or that he's a bit queasy. Or maybe he sighs deeply once or twice, and that causes him to have difficulty catching his next breath. He feels off-kilter, not quite right.

For others, the cycle starts with certain behaviors. Mary, let's say, comes to believe that she or her parent will be in danger if she isn't carrying her lucky My Little Pony Fluttershy doll. One day, she realizes she's accidentally left it at home, and her anxiety spikes. Or Johnny, suffering from social anxiety, won't go to the school dance.

For each of these children, the cycle is under way.

How Thoughts, Feelings, and Behaviors Interact

The three components often work together to maintain anxiety. For example, your child is invited to a birthday party and she feels nervous about attending. On the way to her friend's house, you explain that you'll be back to pick her up in three hours. Three hours sounds like a very long time to her, three hours when she won't see you. She may start thinking to herself: *What if mom forgets to come back in time? I'm scared.* As a result of her thoughts, she develops butterflies in her stomach and her hands feel jiggly. She may at that point exhibit a separation behavior, saying, "I don't want to go to this party. I just want to go home."

And perhaps she gets to skip the party. Avoidant behaviors, in turn, contribute to negative cognitions; the anxious thoughts are reinforced. The next time a party comes around, it's even harder for your child. She begins to believe she isn't able to go to parties, since she was unsuccessful the last time. It's simply beyond her capabilities.

The cycle is maintained.

We teach parents to fit information into our "Cycle of Anxiety" handout based on what they have observed in their child. We try to figure out where anxiety typically takes hold, which element triggers the others and whips the child's fears into something bigger and scarier. Then we consider the best way to interrupt the cycle so it doesn't feed on itself; we talk about the kinds of thought-changing or feeling-changing or behavior-changing skills that will be good for the child to master.

You may find this process extremely helpful. Using the three-component model, spend some time reflecting on the situations that seem to give your child trouble, in how matters start and how they escalate. Viewing anxiety in general terms—saying "Just relax, take it easy, stop worrying"—never works very well, as you've probably learned. Once you look at anxiety as a three-part cycle, on the other hand, you become a much more effective coach for your child.

Examining thoughts, accepting feelings, and changing behaviors are the subjects of the following three chapters, where I'll explain particular intervention strategies to break into the cycle. Add these to your parenting tool kit to go along with the five-minutes-a-day child-directed special time that you've established and the soothing and predictable sleep routine you've instigated.

CHAPTER 7

Examining Anxious Thoughts

One Step in Breaking the Cycle

We all like to believe what we think. We like to believe that what we think is true. Yet we adults realize that some of what we think isn't entirely true or even necessarily true at all. Anxious children, however, have trouble with that notion.

In treating a child, I will sometimes use a silly example to demonstrate. Suppose I believed, I say, that my hair will turn green tomorrow. You would know it's very unlikely that I'll wake up with green hair. But suppose I really, really believed I was going to have green hair and I worried about it a whole lot. It would still not happen, don't you agree? The child usually gets the point: I can believe all I want, but that doesn't make it true.

An anxious child may become rigid in his way of thinking, or somewhat biased in his overinterpretation of neutral situations as threatening. The worst-case scenario that he holds in his mind, whatever it is, is the only possible truth. Because he thinks it, it must be so. Stopping stressful thoughts through cognitive restructuring—changing the way you think about things— disrupts the cycle of anxiety at its start for many kids.

The techniques I'll describe will encourage your child to evaluate and replace maladaptive thoughts, which is largely a matter of generating new, more accurate ideas and becoming a little more mentally flexible and realistic. Anxious kids usually have a lot of thoughts swirling around, but the youngest ones may not be able to verbalize them, or may even have trouble identifying them without a parent's help. Older children may be able to identify thoughts but not know how to change them. Mom and dad play a critical role.

Cognitive restructuring is not simply pulling out a negative thought and sticking in a happy one. In fact, it's not a simple process at all. Our natural and understandable instinct as parents might be to tell a fearful child, "Well, that's just not going to happen, you don't have to worry" or "Whatever gave you that idea? Forget about it." We might try to jolly her out of her fears. We might find her fears and concerns so outlandish or off the wall that we can't imagine where they came from — and why she won't just snap out of it.

Changing thoughts takes some time and patience and empathetic understanding on your part. You want your child to go through the steps of carefully examining how what she thinks is making her anxious and unhappy, usually for no reason. Here's how to begin the process.

Thinking about Thinking

Before introducing cognitive restructuring skills, you may need to open a dialogue with your child about thoughts in general.

If he is under age 7, it may be hard for him to say what he's thinking; in many cases he's not cognitively ready to do that. You'll probably have more success talking about feelings. In addition, it's often easier for kids to discuss someone else's thoughts, rather than their own. Some simple visual aids can be useful in extracting ideas.

To help a youngster figure out what a thought is, I cut pictures from magazines of people's faces—feeling faces. We look at them. That lady is smiling, she looks happy. Here's a picture of a little boy who seems sad. What's going on with the lady or the boy? I'll ask.

The child might say, "He's sad because he just broke his bicycle." "The lady is smiling because she left work and she's going home and later she's going to the movies." Why else could the boy be sad? What else might be making the lady happy and feeling good? We'll come up with a number of possibilities, and then we've arrived at the concept that there are many reasons one can be sad or happy and many thoughts that could lead to those emotions. I use one cartoon picture that shows a little girl biting her nails, a worried frown on her face, with two empty thought bubbles over her head; we discuss how to fill in the bubbles, what might be going on in her mind that's making her bite her nails.

Once we've generated the concept, I'll ask, Have you ever had thoughts that made you happy? The child says, "It makes me happy when I think about my birthday next month and I'm going to get presents." Or he's thinking about his pet hamster or the time his dad took him to the amusement park and they went on all the rides. What thoughts made you sad? "I saw a picture of a polar bear who didn't have enough ice to stand on, and it made me very sad."

Parents use photos of their child. One mother and her daughter flipped through the family album that included a lot of pictures of birthday parties past. "Annie was very interested in a picture from her fourth birthday, showing the table with all the kids having cake," said this parent, "and Annie was not looking pleased at all. I asked her if she remembered what she was feeling right then, and she did. She told me she was annoyed because she thought this one girl, Maddy, was hogging all the attention and talking about the neat stuff everybody did at *her* party."

This little technique helps kids flesh out the idea and make the connection that what we are thinking causes us to have different emotions; thoughts have an effect on how we feel. For anxious children, it's the beginning of a critical lesson: if we can change the way we think, we can also sometimes change the way we feel and the way we act.

Probability Overestimation and Catastrophizing

The two most common kinds of anxiety thinking are probability overestimation (*something I won't like is definitely going to happen*) and catastrophizing (*when it happens it will be an absolute disaster and I won't be able to cope at all*). They tend to go together. (*If I take the train, I will go crazy and my body will explode or my heart will go so fast that it will beat right out of my chest and I'll do something that people will think is nuts.*)

Here's an example from a young girl who experienced a great deal of separation anxiety. When Andrea, age 11, was waiting to be picked up by her mom or dad from school or a friend's house, or waiting for them to arrive home from work or from an evening out, she began worrying if they were a tiny bit late, even just five minutes. Her immediate thought was that her parent had been killed in a car crash.

She couldn't say just where the fear came from or when it started. Maybe she saw something bad on TV, she suggested, and that put the idea in her mind. But whenever her parents weren't where they were supposed to be, she'd dwell and obsess on it and call them numerous times on her cell phone. If they were meeting friends for dinner, she'd beg them to tell her exactly when they were going to get in the car to head for home, and then calculate the number of minutes it would take from when they left to when they should arrive. When once she was unable to reach her mother on her phone, she burst into tears. It was true, she believed; there had been an accident, her parents were dead. What would happen to her now?

Andrea had another problem. "When they are a little late," I asked, "or you're not sure when to expect them, is there anything you can do to make yourself feel a bit better?" She said no, never, she's too upset, her stomach always hurts. This young girl was worrying about worrying! The amount she worried spun her into a hugely worked-up state.

We discussed how she could take a closer look at her worry thoughts. We began searching for evidence that her thoughts were probably true or probably not true.

The last time your parents were late, I asked, did they get into a car accident? *No.*

Have they ever been in a car accident? *No.*

Do you know other people who sometimes came late and didn't get into a car accident? *Yes.*

What are some reasons you might not be able to reach Mom on her phone? *Maybe her batteries died, but she didn't.*

What are some reasons besides being in a car accident that they might be late? What possibilities can you think of?

Andrea started searching in a logical way for any other explanation, as a detective might. She quickly began coming up with new thoughts that were more consistent with her evidence.

Maybe there was a lot of traffic. If it's 5:00, there's a lot of commuters going back and forth. Maybe Mom and Dad ran out of gas. They stayed later to talk to someone.

Then the second step: Even if mom is late, I asked, could you handle it? I encouraged Andrea to think of positive actions she could take instead of stewing silently and miserably with her overwhelming fears.

I could stay with another parent. I'd stay with the coach until Mom got to soccer practice to pick me up. There will always be somebody there. No one will leave me alone.

This young girl was generating ideas she could use the next time she felt herself starting to worry without obvious cause. That's the heart of cognitive restructuring.

Probability overestimation and catastrophizing can flare up in a number of ways, and these particular subcategories, so to speak, of maladaptive thinking are often associated with one or another of the anxiety disorders I described in chapter 2. As you help your child develop better, more accurate thoughts, you might recognize one of the following mental patterns.

Mind Reading

In theory-of-mind studies, it's been noted that children over the age of, roughly, 4 or 5 are able to recognize that other people have thoughts that may differ from their own.

In one classic demonstration of a "false-belief task," a group of youngsters watch two girls, Sally and Anne, in a room. Sally has a basket and a small ball or marble. Anne has a box. Sally places the marble in her basket and leaves the room, whereupon Anne removes the marble and puts it in her box. Sally returns. The children observing this scene are asked, Where will Sally look for the marble?

Some kids say Sally will look for it in the box, because they know that's where it is. Others, realizing what they know but Sally doesn't, say she'll look in her basket, where she left it. This group understands Sally's thinking and accurately predicts her behavior.

An anxious child in the mind-reading category believes that, first, she knows what someone else is thinking; second, that person is thinking the same way she is; and third, these thoughts will cause the person to behave or respond in a negative manner.

Joni, a 9-year-old with a sophisticated sense of humor, refused to speak to anyone she considered a stranger, including the pleasant next-door neighbor, clerks in grocery stores, and substitute teachers in her third-grade classroom. Joni's concerned mother said, "She says it's because she's afraid they'll think what she says is stupid. But it's embarrassing when she won't acknowledge someone who says hello to her." Joni's worry over how others would perceive her was causing her self-confidence to collapse and her rejecting behaviors to make people view her as unfriendly.

I suggested to Joni's mother that she help her daughter recognize how she was mind reading by asking her about her own thought process when someone spoke to her. For example, "Are you waiting for Mrs. White next door to say something stupid each time she says 'hello' to you?"

Joni smiled at this and said, "Of course not."

"Why do you think she's waiting for *you* to say something stupid?"

Joni shrugged, admitting that it was, in fact, unlikely the neighbor was expecting her to sound dumb.

Once Joni began to see the flaws in her thinking, her mom set up some simple challenges to help her become braver about speaking to people she didn't know well. The girl tried ordering pizza over the phone, taking the change from a clerk in a store and saying "Thank you," and saying "Hello" when she and her mom saw the neighbor. She learned that "Hello" wasn't going to lead to a long conversation that she wasn't prepared for, and she started to relax and didn't freeze up when a stranger spoke to her.

Joseph, a young teen who occasionally experienced panic attacks, believed that when another boy in class was looking at him, that kid didn't like what Joseph was saying and probably didn't much like Joseph in general. What particularly worried Joseph was that anyone seeing him in a panicky state would think he was crazy and tell everyone else about it.

We talked about other reasons a classmate might glance in his direction. Maybe that fellow was lost in his own thoughts about something that had nothing to do with Joseph? We talked about the likelihood that people could recognize his panic. Suppose, I asked him, I was sweating right now and my heart was racing and I was short of breath. Would you know I was having a panic attack, unless you actually saw drips coming down my face and heard me gasping? Probably not, he admitted.

With a child caught in mind-reading anxieties, I sometimes offer a small demonstration, testing out the theory that others are perhaps not all that interested in oneself. We'll go to Faneuil Hall Marketplace, a promenade in downtown Boston where many people gather for lunch and to enjoy the waterfront, or go to a park. Watch what happens, I say, and then I run up the stairs or out on the grass and twirl around with my arms outstretched. After, I ask the child to tell me how many people were looking at me. In fact, maybe one or two glanced for a second, then returned to their lunch or conversation. Nobody paid much attention. The kid usually cracks up about it all, and starts to recognize, *Well, yeah, not everybody is focused on me. Maybe I'm overestimating the probability that many people are sitting around watching me and thinking I'm crazy. And even if they were, what's the big deal? So maybe I shouldn't obsess so much about what people think.*

Fortune-Telling

Children with generalized anxiety are often great fortune-tellers, certain that they can predict what's going to happen, and what's going to happen will be the end of the world. Generalized anxiety disorder (GAD) is *super*-future-oriented. Nothing has actually occurred yet or did occur in the past to suggest that it will, but the child is anticipating impending doom. GAD is very much in the mind, whereas with other anxieties, the focus is more specific or on objects—dogs, bugs, social encounters, separation.

Like Eddie, the boy in chapter 2 whose parents called him "the house policeman," these children typically have a laundry list of negative thoughts: *Is there enough food in the house for dinner? Suppose it rains on our vacation? Where is the nearest hospital? Can we afford to move?*

The catastrophizing element is huge. For example, many kids with this kind of erroneous thinking brood constantly about their own health or the health of their family members. One child and his parents and siblings had dinner at McDonald's. On the way home, mom said she had a little stomachache. For days afterward, the boy imagined the worst (she had cancer, she was going to die). His mom said she felt fine, she probably had just had too much to eat. He was not reassured.

With a fortune-telling youngster, I talk about the fact that none of us can really predict the future, or perhaps can do so in only limited ways. I'll have the child write down all his worry thoughts, and then we methodically go through the list to try to figure out which are thinking errors and which might be worth a tiny bit of worrying but not that much.

Black-and-White Thinking

Some anxious children view the world in all-or-nothing, black-and-white terms, also called "dichotomous thinking." *If I don't make an A on everything, I'm a complete failure. If I give that speech and flub one word, the speech is no good. Either I'm popular or I'm not. People either like me or hate me.* With reality testing, they begin to allow room for a little gray in the middle.

Do you need to be popular? If you have a couple of close friends, is your life still okay?

Amanda, an eighth grader, had trouble staying awake in class. Her teacher noticed that the girl seemed to "space out" a lot. Amanda was a good student, although sometimes slower than the others to complete her classwork; her homework was always done on time and exceptionally neat.

The teacher's first thought was that this kid was simply not getting enough sleep, and at a conference, she asked the girl's parents if their daughter had a reasonable bedtime. She learned that Amanda consistently stayed up late doing homework, and in fact, her parents were concerned because eighth grade seemed so challenging for her. They were considering having her evaluated for an undetected learning disorder. Her father had also been questioning the wisdom of keeping their child enrolled in a school in which the teacher was apparently assigning upwards of four hours of homework each night.

What they missed was Amanda's extreme anxiety over getting her work "just right." She never gave herself permission to make a mistake; she overdid all her assignments. If one was to read a particular section of a book, Amanda felt she must read and try to remember every word (including the foreword, table of contents, copyright notice, and so on) and wouldn't go to bed until she had. Then she'd obsess about whether she'd read it all, whether she should get up early to rewrite her papers, whether she'd done everything right.

The teacher was shocked. All the adults could see that this child was exhausted and struggling to keep up in school, but none had any idea it was because anxiety was causing her to overdo it.

We led Amanda through a reality checklist, looking for evidence that maybe it wasn't necessary for her to work so hard:

Did all the other kids in class do as much homework?

Had she ever before received a good grade without rewriting her work?

Did her teacher actually require this much work, or was she imposing it on herself?

Restructuring her thoughts, Amanda started to get better, though turning things around didn't happen quickly. It was difficult for this child to let herself go to sleep at night knowing she hadn't read and memorized every piece of her assignments.

Magical Thinking

"Thought-action fusion" refers to the tendency to believe that thinking about an action is the same as doing it. Children and teens with obsessive-compulsive disorder often engage in this kind of faulty, essentially magical thinking. I coached one 16-year-old, Kate, whose obsessions and compulsions were causing her great distress.

She had lost her mother a year earlier and was terrified that something bad would happen to her father. Her dad brought her to the clinic because he felt increasingly puzzled by her behavior; she was oppositional, she didn't listen to him. He related this story. They drove up to a pizza shop where he had earlier called in an order, and asked Kate to go in and pick up the food. She refused. Dad said, "Look, there are no parking spots here. Just run in and get our stuff and come back." Kate would not; she sat in the car. This was the incident that finally caused her father, in frustration and anger, to seek therapy for her.

Kate and I talked about this and several similar instances that had annoyed her dad, and eventually she explained that she had not gone into the shop for the food because she would have been unable to do it three times. "He didn't order three pizzas," she said. "I couldn't get out of the car three times. I feel like I have to do things three times or something bad will happen to him." She hadn't mentioned this compulsion to her father. She thought it might be a little weird and was embarrassed. And he had absolutely no clue what was in his daughter's mind. When he learned, he was stunned.

Kate described all the rituals she had to repeat three times each in the course of a day. She wasn't sure when it started, but the behaviors had been going on for most of the past year. Often, the thought-action connection comes about innocuously and accidentally. Perhaps leaving one morning, she forgot items she needed for school and had to go back inside three times to collect them. And the rest of that day turned out to be a good one. This is how magical thinking can take hold: *If something good happens, it's linked to a behavior of mine. I remember going in and out three times. Therefore I can prevent something bad from happening by doing things three times.* This in turn evolved into overestimating the likelihood that something bad absolutely *would* happen if she failed to perform her rituals.

Cognitive restructuring for a child with obsessive-compulsive disorder takes a somewhat unique form. I might have the child consider whether a thought is true or not true, or whether she might be overestimating the possibility that it is true. She's encouraged to think about where it came from and why it somehow "stuck." But the most effective strategy is to have the child with OCD raise the troubling thought in her mind and sit with it without performing the anxiety-relieving compulsions she has adopted.

Though it caused her a great deal of anxiety, we were able to get Kate to the point of stopping her repetitive actions. She acknowledged that she did, nevertheless, have a decent day, her father didn't die, and everything turned out pretty much all right. Then we helped her to see that even if something negative or upsetting did occur, it wasn't because of a thought or an action she had or had not taken. With her father's understanding and support, she got better. At the end, we had them repeat the scene: dad ordered a pizza; Kate left the car—one time—picked up the pizza, and came back. All went well.

Sometimes we suggest that a child externalize the obsessive thought and "talk back" to it: *OCD, take a hike, I don't need to listen to you.* Some children give it a name, often the name of a kid they don't like. One girl said, "I want to call it Stacy—she is a mean bully at my school—because it will remind me that I shouldn't be listening to Stacy." Just the name itself annoyed her and helped her to feel stronger and decide she would not give in to Stacy-OCD.

Another child, 13-year-old Simon, had a series of repetitive behaviors and rituals he had to practice in the morning. I asked him to imagine his anxiety as a person or thing and give it a name, and he decided it was a funny-looking creature called "The Spinyman" who sat on his left shoulder. We encouraged him to talk back to the Spinyman, laying out the facts of the matter.

Simon learned to tell the Spinyman that it was fine to go to school, because the likelihood of his house burning down while he was out was actually quite small, especially since his family had working smoke detectors and lived a couple blocks from the local fire station. Externalizing the thought helped Simon cope with irrational fears that were driving his compulsive behaviors.

Coping Cards for Brave Thoughts

This is a simple strategy to help your child change her anxious worry thoughts into better ones. The two of you together — or she can do this on her own, if she's old enough and she wants to — will write down brave statements, her personal coping cards to carry with her.

Get a pack of index cards and cut from them a number of smaller cards, about 3 inches by 2 inches or so. Index cards are fairly stiff and will hold up through use, which is good; at the same time, the smaller rectangles are not so obvious to anyone else. If you produce a bunch of cards, put a hole through the upper left corners of the cards and tie them together with a piece of ribbon or run a binder ring through them.

In an anxious moment, a glance at her written-down thoughts can remind your child to "talk to herself" in a more positive way. Kids love coping cards. They put them in their backpacks and pull them out, perhaps surreptitiously, during the day for a little reinforcement, a personal pep talk.

Here are a few sample "brave thoughts" that I have used for various children's coping cards:

- I can think of a happy time in my life when I felt strong and brave.
- Most of the time, people won't even be able to tell I'm nervous.
- I can sleep by myself without feeling scared.
- I can deal with whatever comes my way.
- I can remember trying hard in the past and succeeding.
- Before getting angry, I can count to 10 and relax and then say how I feel.
- I can have fun. I do not need to worry about everything.
- Speaking up in class helps everyone learn.
- I can say nice things to myself to make myself feel happy.
- It's okay to make mistakes or ask silly questions.

Some of these may be especially appropriate to your child's circumstances. Or help her create her own coping thoughts relating to the particular situations that bring on anxious feelings. You might encourage her to remember stressful moments in the past and how she got through them. That may suggest useful coping thoughts for the future: "When I feel nervous, I can still answer questions in class and do okay." "I can think of something kind to say to another kid while we're lining up for lunch."

Playing Detective

As the examples I've described demonstrate, cognitive restructuring is partly playing detective, seeking information to determine if a thought is true or not true. We start from the position that each worry thought is a guess, not a fact. And so we must look around for some facts.

When I work with a child, I'll sometimes mark four columns on a piece of paper. I might draw a little magnifying glass on the top, to remind her that we're being detectives and searching for clues.

In the first column, the child, with my help, writes down the anxious or negative thought in her mind.

In the second column, she writes down any evidence or facts to support that the thought is true.

In the third column, she writes down any evidence or facts to support that the thought is false.

If the "false" column is longer than the "true" column, we toss the thought away and in column four write down a new, adaptive thought that is more consistent with the facts.

To come up with evidence, the child asks herself a number of questions, looking a little more critically at her thoughts and considering alternative explanations. It's a process of countering probability overestimations and de-catastrophizing:

Do I know for sure that _____ will happen?

What evidence do I have that _____ will happen?

How likely is it really?

Has _____ ever happened before?

Am I absolutely certain of these awful consequences?

Do I have a crystal ball?

And then:

Even if _____ happens, can I live through it?

What is the worst possible outcome? How bad is that?

Could I cope?

Do I know anyone else who has been in this situation? What did they do?

Have I been able to cope with _____ in the past?

Is it really so terrible?

In another exercise, I draw two circles that look like pies. I say to the child, "You're worrying about [parents not coming home, whatever the issue is]. Show me how much you're worrying." Typically, the child marks off a giant slice of the first pie. After we conduct our due diligence and gather information about the actual probability of this event taking place, we look at the second pie, and I say, "Draw for me how much you now think you should be worrying." The child usually gets excited about making the tiniest dot he can imagine, like a crumb. The real chance this thing will happen is so slight that he probably should worry just about that much.

I'm encouraging the child to stop and think, to use his mind in a way that's consistent with the truth, rather than in a way that's skewed and only going to cause more anxiety for no reason.

This kind of concrete representation of "a lot of worrying" versus "a little tiny bit of worrying" tends to be effective with very young children, whose cognitive strengths are still limited. One boy, 5-year-old Alexander, had developed some hives after eating at a picnic. His doctor said the reaction indicated a slight sensitivity to sesame seeds on a hamburger bun, nothing to be overly concerned about, but Alex should stay away from them. His parents, not overly concerned, took some reasonable precautions. But Alex went totally crazy.

At the time his mother brought him to the clinic, the child was avoiding most foods, afraid of "seeds." He was suspicious of everything, from ketchup on up. He wouldn't eat in a restaurant, wouldn't eat anything but yogurt and hot dogs without buns, and had lost a significant amount of weight. His mom had started giving him nutritional supplement shakes to keep his energy up. Alex was also asking many questions every day, which had begun to grate on his parents' nerves. He demanded to know where each item of food came from, what store it had been bought at, what was in it, and so on.

I suggested to Alex's mother that she not "overexplain" to him that his fears were unfounded, but with our help the boy was able to figure out the probability that he would accidentally ingest sesame seeds. "If your mom packs your lunch for you every day so you know what's in it," we asked, "and you can very easily avoid a roll with sesame seeds, what are the chances you'll eat one?" He realized the chance of this happening was very small. He responded with some glee to the "worry pie," marking off the tiny amount of worrying he would do. This was a step forward. I also recommended that Alex's mom find some kind of fun reward to entice him to be a more adventurous eater. She decided to reinforce

Alex's brave choices by using a "new food bell"—a tiny gong that she found in Boston's Chinatown—to signal a successful try. A week or two later, she reported that her son enjoyed seeing that if he tried a new food, she would leap up and ring the bell.

At the end of the month, his mom said that when he was offered a special treat for his brave eating behavior at home, Alex asked his parents to take him out to a restaurant. "I can go to any restaurant," he said confidently, "as long as I tell them I can't eat sesame seeds."

Exploring "real chances" is a useful tool with youngsters, and it's one I often use with kids who worry about intruders coming into their home. "It hasn't happened yet," the child says, "but I saw it once on the news." "Well, the news told you about the one time it happened," I reply, "but not about the ten million times it didn't happen." We decide the real chance is pretty slim after all.

With an older child, we might talk about the probability that the worrisome thing will occur. Is it really 100 percent? Or maybe there's a 60 percent or 10 percent chance. If the child is seriously overestimating, and basing his fear on misinformation, that's the beginning of helping him restructure his thoughts.

At stressful moments, many children get themselves into a lot of heated emotion immediately, especially with generalized anxiety, in which the thoughts are coming incessantly. Parents have told me, "Well, it would be terrific if he could just stop and think, but he's too worked up at that point." For most kids, practicing thought-changing techniques when they're calm and focused is successful. In an anxiety-provoking situation, then, the child can remember—or a parent or clued-in teacher who's on the scene perhaps can remind him—*I should use my detective skills right now.*

Practicing is so beneficial. After a while, the process becomes second nature. He doesn't have to write it all out. He can do it in his head.

See if you can engage your child in a thought-changing discussion at a time she mentions her fear. One 12-year-old, Colleen, was terrified of speaking in front of her class because she had a tendency to blush and her hands shook. Several avoidance behaviors had been taking root, which was a concern to Colleen's parents and to her teacher. Here's a conversation her mother initiated.

Colleen: Mom, I don't want to go to school today. It's class presentation day, and probably the teacher will call on me to talk.

Mom: What's so bad about talking in front of the class?

Colleen: I start blushing and everyone will see my neck and my face getting red, and my hands getting shaky.

Mom: Have you ever given one of these presentations before and turned red?

Colleen: I don't really know, but I always feel my face getting hot and my stomach is nervous.

Mom: Do other kids in class feel nervous about speaking?

Colleen: Some kids do. Not everybody.

Mom: So some kids feel just like you do. Have you ever seen someone else whose face got red or who was shaky when they spoke in front of the group?

Colleen: My friend Elizabeth blushes a lot when she talks. I don't think it bothers her, though.

Mom: Does anyone comment on it?

Colleen: No, I've never heard anyone say anything.

Mom: So maybe it's possible that you will speak and you'll blush and no one will say anything or think twice about it?

Colleen: Yeah, I guess that's possible.

Mom: Sounds to me like you're focusing a lot on what people will think, but probably your classmates have other things on their minds. What else could your friends be thinking about when you speak?

Colleen: They could be thinking about what I'm saying. Or probably they're thinking about what they're going to do after school. *(Laughs.)*

Mom: You know, even if some kids did notice that you were shaky or your face was red, would that be so terrible, something you could never get over?

Colleen: Well, no, of course not, I'd get over it. Most likely it would bother me a lot until class was over, but I'd forget about it.

As they continued their talk, Colleen's mother pointed out that lots of people get pre-speech jitters; that anxious feelings and bodily sensations are normal, but they do go away; and that negative thoughts just take focus away from the task at hand. Colleen wrote out a thought-changing list:

My nervous thoughts
I'm going to blush when I get up in front of the class.
Everyone will see me blushing and make fun of me later.
Everyone will see my hands shaking.
I'm going to mess up my speech.

Facts to support that the thoughts are true
The fact is that I do blush.

Facts to support that the nervous thoughts are not true
I have given a talk a couple of times before and it went okay.
Nobody has ever said anything about me getting red in the
    face or has called me names.
Other kids mess up sometimes, and no one seems to care.
    Usually everyone claps no matter how the person did.

If someone did notice or made fun of me, would it be the end of the world?

No, it wouldn't be a catastrophe, like something that causes death or illness. Even if someone did say something, I could just say, "Hey, at least I got up and did it." I could also ignore any rude comments. I guess I have ways to cope.

Easing the Pressure

Will your child willingly and gratefully want to sit down with you and analyze his worries? Maybe not. If you say "Let's make a list of all the anxious thoughts you're having and figure out which ones are true or false," will that seem like a welcome task to him? Or will it feel like a chore, more homework? Saying "Here's a sheet of paper, you're going to write down your thoughts now" could sound boring, too cut-and-dried, or maybe slightly alarming.

See how you can make the cognitive restructuring effort a little more creative and a little more fun. The format of how to teach and encourage a child can be anything that works and that a child finds acceptable. Parents often invent their own ways to help their child first notice that he's having a worry thought and then use his skills to change it.

Here are several ideas.

The Worry Bag

Use a plain bag that your child can decorate, or a gift bag from a card store. He writes a worry thought on a piece of paper or an index card, restructures it mentally, and writes the more positive, adaptive thought on the other side. He puts the card in the worry bag.

It's a kind of physical trick, making the anxious thought *go* somewhere, getting it away, out of his head. Some parents have come up with a box that's like a treasure chest with a clasp, so the thought appears to have been locked away. It's in a safe place where the child doesn't have to think about it anymore. Many young kids take to this idea. Seeing a filled-up worry bag is a tangible reminder of their accomplishment.

Then you might notice how many times your child has restructured anxious thoughts on his own, without prompting or nagging, which is all to the good. If he's restructured three thoughts over the course of a day, mom can say, "Look how great you've done. You're learning not to worry so much." Maybe he gets a reward.

A Game of Catch

Many kids have a hard time paying attention. Sitting down and doing something on paper just doesn't feel consistent with their nature or with their age. We might get the thoughts flowing by using a soft fabric ball I keep in my office. I'll think of a worry thought and say it out loud: "If I go to the party, no one will want to talk to me." I toss the ball across to the child.

When he catches it, he has to say what kind of thinking error was involved in my statement. I say, "Excellent, you recognized that I was fortune-telling, predicting the future. Now you tell me one."

Say the Secret Word

Devise a code word, an agreed-upon signal from parent to child that he's spiraling into anxious thinking. It's a bit embarrassing, after all, with a peer driving in the car, say, to bring up, "You're starting to obsess again, you know what to do." Instead, mom or dad says a funny word or uses it in an innocent-sounding sentence: "Let's have *macaroni* later." "Shall we get *hot cocoa?*" The child remembers, *Oh yeah,* macaroni *means remember to use my detective skills. That's right. Find a thought that will make me feel better right now.*

Modeling

Suppose you and your family are driving to an appointment, you're running late, there doesn't seem to be any place to park the car. Voice your thoughts. "I'm worried we'll never find a parking spot. We'll be so late. But you know what I'm thinking now? It'll be fine. We might have to leave the car a few blocks away and walk. It won't be the worst thing in the world."

Suppose a storm is coming, and the TV meteorologist is talking about downed power lines. Say, "This doesn't sound good. We might lose electricity. I hope not. I hope the lights don't go out. But not a big deal. We've got flashlights and candles. We'll manage."

Just talk out loud. You let your child hear a worry concern that's on your mind and then hear you restructure the thought. It doesn't have to be fake or strained. Just naturally model adaptive thinking.

Passing on Successes

At the end of treatment with a child, one of my colleagues makes a "commercial," videotaping the youngster talking about what he has learned and how he's changed his worry thoughts. He understands that he has a good message to pass on to other kids who may be coping with similar anxiety issues. The idea of teaching is so powerful. I will sometimes have a child write a letter. "If you knew another kid who was afraid of exactly what you've been afraid of," I say, "what would you encourage him to do? What skill do you think would work?" Putting a child in that helping position can often secure his progress, and it also makes him feel terrific.

For many or even most children, changing thoughts first makes sense. For others, cognitive skills don't seem to be terribly useful. A child might be able to think realistically and restructure all he wants in my office. But we'll see that he is unable to summon up his detective skills in the moment of stress, when he needs them. Confronting the upsetting situation, he goes right into a tailspin— tears, panicky behaviors. He's wound up as tight as a drum.

For these kids, I focus first on physical feelings. One child, for example, was terrified of lightning. His mother said that when a thunder and lighting storm hit, he was unable to use any thinking strategies. For him, relaxation skills, which I describe in the following chapter, worked well. In fact, they're excellent tools for all anxious children if used at the right time.

CHAPTER 8

Accepting Physical Feelings

Learning about the Body

When I give a talk to a group of parents, one of my favorite intro-ductory activities is having them participate in what is called an "interoceptive exposure exercise," during which they intention-ally bring about some of the heightened physical sensations asso-ciated with anxiety disorders.

I ask my audience members to stand up and jog in place for two minutes. This is usually somewhat unpleasant for them to do. It's unpleasant for me to do, but we all keep at it for our required two minutes. I then ask them to shout out the symptoms they notice. Someone says, "Well, I'm sweaty." Another: "I'm out of breath." "My heart is beating really fast." I reply, "Let me know when your heartbeat seems to come back down to a normal rate." Within a minute or so, almost all hands are raised. "Now we're going to do another exercise," I say.

I have my audience members turn their heads from side to side for thirty seconds. And again they will tell me what they are experiencing: "Dizzy." "That made me kind of light-headed." I ask them to raise their hands once the feelings have resolved.

Within about thirty seconds, three-quarters of the hands are in the air; within one minute, everyone reports being back to normal.

One final exercise involves breathing through little cocktail straws while holding their noses closed. Their shout-outs: "I can hardly breathe." "You can't suck in enough air." Again the sensations resolve within a minute or so.

As all are sitting down with relief, I talk a little about what they felt. They were able to name their symptoms and clearly associated them with the exercises. The heart rate increases as it does when we go for a run. But we're not frightened by it because we've purposely brought it on. We know why it's there. Similarly, we're not frightened by the light-headedness or the relative lack of air in our lungs.

These are exactly the kinds of feelings that anxious children experience. But imagine that you're 12 years old and in a classroom and suddenly your heart is hammering, you can't catch your breath, you feel dizzy, and you don't know why. How terrifying it can be for a child or teen who might not have any idea what is going on in her body. "I want you to notice," I tell my audience, "how quickly our bodies knew how to bring us back down to homeostasis, or balance. The panicking 12-year-old doesn't realize that. She wants to escape. She worries that something terrible is about to take place."

"Unbalanced" physical feelings are frightening when we're unaware of why they're happening or we're not in control of them. But they are the result of natural emotions and are no reason for alarm. This is what anxious children need to be helped to understand.

The exercises I put my parent audiences through are similar to those we do in treatment with kids who experience panic or other anxiety expressions. They observe that their bodies resolve the symptoms within a short time. I explain that the body will respond in the exact same way during a panic attack if the child allows it to.

If your child is terribly upset by the physical sensations associated with a panic attack, you can lead her through an interoceptive exposure exercise at home, so she begins to learn that what we feel doesn't have to scare us. Later in this chapter, I'll explain how to design one. You might also talk with her about how the body works.

Basic Body Lessons

Most kids find it comforting to understand *why* they experience certain physical sensations when they're frightened, and that these feelings are actually quite normal. In getting across this message to your child, help her see that anxiety is a natural emotion and the response it evokes is evolutionary, as I described in chapter 2. Because anxious kids so often believe they're the only ones to have such sensations, and usually worry that there must be something very wrong, it's important to stress that all animals and people are hard-wired in this way. Here is a suggested explanation (to convey in age-appropriate language):

"You're giving a talk in front of the class, let's say, and you're afraid you won't do it well. Some kids will laugh or say something bad about you. You're starting to sweat, your mouth is dry, your stomach is upset, your face feels hot and flushed. This rush of symptoms is your body's protective mechanism kicking into gear. Somehow you've told yourself that you're in a state of danger, and you're preparing for it.

"Each one of the physical feelings that comes up is adaptive, meaning it's designed to keep you from harm. When your body is covered in sweat, for example, it would be harder for a threatening beast to try to grab you. Why does your heart race? If you were really in trouble, you'd need more blood to get to your legs so that you could run away fast if you had to. Stomach feels funny? It would not be adaptive in a situation of danger to stop and pick up a burger to eat. Your body automatically shuts down production in your stomach so that you won't feel hungry. Typically, once the source of danger is over, you feel hungry again.

"You're afraid you'll faint? Well, no, you won't. In fact, when you're anxious your blood pressure rises, and fainting is the opposite of what happens. Afraid you will throw up? Highly unlikely. If you were in danger, it would not be adaptive to stop and vomit.

"Ironically, when you are building to a panic attack, you are the safest you can be because your entire system is ready to respond to anything."

Older kids can grasp that this state of "high alert," when channeled productively, is what allows athletes to win competitions and actors to step outside of their own personas and believably channel their characters. It's what enables game show contestants to hit the answer buzzer faster than anyone else.

Knowing her body is programmed to—*supposed to*—respond is a huge relief to an anxious youngster. Then she needs to know that her body, all on its own and usually within just a few minutes, will resolve the intense and worrisome feelings.

In chapter 6, I described 13-year-old Becca, who was prone to anxiety attacks and had a desperate need to hear her mother's voice in order to calm herself. When she started to panic, she immediately felt her heart begin to pound and had to struggle to catch her breath. She was convinced that the sensations that overtook her meant she was going to throw up, faint, or possibly die.

During our treatment, I helped Becca induce and stay with

the symptoms that were so upsetting to her. We'd begin when she was in a relaxed and controlled environment, not experiencing any distress. I coached her through exercises—for example, doing jumping jacks or breathing through a straw—to bring on the same physical sensations that she associated with her attacks, which she then rated on an anxiety intensity scale of 0 to 8, with 8 representing the extreme.

When she reached the edge of what she felt she could tolerate—at first, a 4 or 5 on her anxiety scale—she would sit while I used a stopwatch to time how long it took for her body to regulate. Once Becca realized her heart slowed down and her breathing returned to normal after only a minute or two, she was able to acknowledge and confront those same sensations during a panic attack.

To help Gabe, a boy who was terribly afraid of dogs, his mom reminded him that he might start to shake or feel his heart beating hard whenever they saw a dog. She coached him to avoid the urge to cross the street and to realize that the symptoms quickly went away. Gabe learned to give himself an anxiety intensity rating on the scale of 0 to 8. He practiced walking by dogs while noticing and experiencing what was happening in his body, and gradually his discomfort dropped from a 5 to a 1 or 2. Before long, he no longer needed his mother's prompting when a dog approached on the street, and he didn't feel nervous at all when passing one behind a fence in a yard.

Here's the point: Anxious kids often rush away from a stressful situation before there is time for heightened physical sensations to resolve naturally. They come to believe that these feelings are to be avoided at all costs. And the costs can be high. I've worked with children who developed excessive avoidance behaviors that caused their lives to be sadly diminished. They'll stay away from sports or exercising or going to the amusement park or even attending school.

Practicing a series of movements that create the feelings they're most afraid of in real life can help tremendously.

Interoceptive Exposure

In carrying out the following exercises, your child induces many of the physical sensations associated with anxiety disorders. She takes note of them and of how her body responds. She becomes an observer rather than a victim of the symptoms she has considered frightening. I've used this technique with kids experiencing all types of anxiety.

When treating a child, we make sure there are no existing medical issues or complications, such as heart problems, fainting, or sudden asthma attacks. For any child in good health, interoceptive exposure exercises pose no difficulties. If you have any concerns, talk to your child's doctor about the exercises. Say: "My kid gets anxious in various situations, and then terribly scared and panicky if her heart starts beating faster or she can't catch her breath. She works herself into a highly overwrought state and has trouble calming down. So we're trying to help her learn that she doesn't have to be afraid of these feelings, they won't hurt her, and that her body will go back to normal very quickly."

Describe how the sensations will be created; explain that this is a time-limited process, thirty seconds to one minute for each movement, just long enough to bring on the sensations in a safe and controlled way. Get the doctor's clearance.

The routine below is similar to what we do in our treatment settings and what you can re-create at home, but in fact, you can achieve the same outcome — or convey the same lesson — through naturalistic exposure, or just hunting up everyday opportunities. Go on a hike with your child, so you both get a little out of breath and your muscles are a bit strained. Some parents I've worked with take their child to a playground where she twirls around on a spin ride or merry-go-round. Some have gone to an amusement park and taken the rides or swings to bring on some dizziness and rapid breathing. Within a family outing, they present the exposure as a kind of fun experiment: "I know you're feeling a little dizzy. Let's see how long it takes for those feelings to go away."

If you follow the controlled process outlined here, you can keep track of progress with your child with this sample record:

Exercise	Sensations	Intensity of Sensation 0–8	Intensity of Anxiety 0–8
• Shake head from side to side for 30 seconds.			
• Place head between legs for 30 seconds. Lift head.			
• Run in place for 1 minute.			
• Hold breath for 30 seconds.			
• Spin in chair for 1 minute.			
• Breathe through straw for 2 minutes.			
• Stare at the light for 1 minute, then read a paragraph.			

Give your child these instructions, in age-appropriate language:

"Do each exercise or movement until you begin to feel physical sensations. Then continue the exercise for another thirty seconds (ten seconds more for holding your breath or head shaking). Remember, you want to bring on those sensations. If you experience only mild sensations after thirty seconds, try to continue the exercise until they reach moderate levels of intensity.

"Focus on the physical feelings. Don't distract yourself. The goal is to learn to be less afraid of these feelings by letting yourself experience them.

"After you stop the exercise, record how intense the physical sensations were (0–8) and how much anxiety you felt. Focus on the physical feelings and watch them come down naturally. When your anxiety is decreased to a mild level (2 or less), record how intense the physical sensations are now (0–8).

"Try to practice each exercise three times in a row each day. Your maximum anxiety level should start to go down with practice as you learn to be less afraid of these feelings."

Preteens and adolescents can do interoceptive exposure on their own, and learn the essential lessons it conveys. *(The sensations I created intentionally are similar to what I feel during a panic attack; just as the sensations went away quickly and naturally during my practice exercise, so they will when I'm panicking.)*

You can be an exercise monitor to a younger child. Tell him to describe what he's feeling. Use a stopwatch, if you want and for dramatic impact, and instruct him to raise his hand when the sensations have gone away or his body feels normal again. Point out that in practically no time at all his heart was no longer beating so fast, his breathing wasn't so hard, his legs didn't hurt, his head wasn't all strange and dizzy, his stomach wasn't sick, his face wasn't flushed and hot. He was fine. He's learning not to let what he feels scare him.

All kids benefit from learning to be more in tune with their bodies. Here's another routine to practice.

Progressive Muscle Relaxation

Children don't really know the difference between "this is how my body feels when it's tense or stressed" and "this is how my body feels when it's relaxed." Everyone should recognize the difference and everyone should learn how to relieve physical tension, which of course we all experience as part of daily life. For anxious kids, and especially those who have trouble with cognitive restructuring or changing their worry thoughts, we've found that practicing relaxation skills can be enormously helpful. Reducing bodily tension often brings on mental benefits as well, a feeling of contentment and confidence. The mind-body connection is a powerful one.

I have developed a series of simple routines—I have recorded these in a CD called *I Can Relax!*—to help children feel the difference between being tense and not tense. In progressive muscle relaxation, the child tightens and releases her muscles, starting with her hands, her shoulders, her face, and so on. She practices slow and easy breathing. She sends her thoughts to a peaceful and happy place. Kids right through middle school age like these exercises. Progressive muscle relaxation is another concrete tool, something they can do to feel in control. Actually, some parents have told me they picked up the practice, too. We all can probably relax more.

The exercises follow, and you might want to record them on an audio tape or your child's iPod so that he can listen and do them as he's lying in bed. Just speak the instructions in a slow, soothing tone of voice. Kids say *I Can Relax!* helps them sleep.

Many also report using it when they especially need to calm down, like the night before a test.

Here's how it goes.

I Can Relax!

Let yourself go to a special place, with no stress, no worries, only peace and relaxation.

Taking Deep Breaths

I want you to breathe in and breathe out, feeling the breath on the back of your throat. In through your nose and out through your mouth. Let's breathe together. Breathe in and breathe out. Take nice deep breaths. Pretend your lungs are little balloons and every time you breathe in, the balloons inflate. Now try taking slower breaths. Breathe in…and breathe out. Breathe in… and breathe out. Notice how your breath feels as it hits the back of your throat. As you slow down your breaths, you begin to feel so nice and relaxed. You're doing a great job.

A Relaxing Place

Try to think of a place that is relaxing to you, where you feel calm and content. What kind of place is relaxing to you? Do you love to sit on the beach? Do you love to sit on a raft in the pool? Do you feel really relaxed in any certain place in your house? Try to think right now of a place that is relaxing to you, where you feel calm and content. Can you think of a relaxing vacation that you took? Try to imagine right now as you take deep, slow breaths, that you are in that relaxing place. Picture yourself there. If you are at the beach, what does the sand feel like? What are you wearing? Is there a cool breeze in the air? What kind of sounds do you hear? Do you hear waves or seagulls?

Are you sitting in front of a crackling fireplace on a cold winter day? Relaxing after playing in the snow? Think of yourself feeling happy, calm, and content. You are sitting in your favorite place and you just had your favorite meal and everyone you love is near you. You have a smile on your face as you breathe in. Picture how happy you are and how good it feels to be relaxed.

The Worry Train

As you sit in your favorite place, notice whether any worries are occupying your thoughts. Suddenly there's a little train that comes by. It has lots of cars and in the back of the train is one large car and that's called the "worry car." That is the car that takes away children's worries. As you take in a deep breath, picture yourself taking each of the worries on your mind and dumping them into the worry car of the train. Make sure you take all of your worries and try to clear your mind of them. Take deep breaths and watch all the worries and nervous thoughts leave your mind. You have no more worries right now because you put them all in the train.

Now the train is going to slowly pull away from the station. Picture what the train looks like as it does so. Watch it as it moves farther and farther away from you. Picture the train getting smaller and smaller as it gets farther and farther away. And watch in your mind as the train takes away all of the worries that were once in your mind. Now you have no more worries, and you have only peaceful, happy, calm thoughts in your mind. You feel nice and comfortable and relaxed. Take a deep breath in and out, and notice how great it feels to have all of those worries out of your mind.

Making Lemonade

As you sit in your relaxing place, picture the sounds you hear. If you're on a beach, you might hear waves or birds. You might also hear kids playing in the sand. You might be on a camping trip, and all you can hear is the sound of crickets in the distance. Or maybe you're lying on a raft in the pool, feeling the warm sun. Wherever you picture yourself, you suddenly find yourself feeling quite thirsty.

You think to yourself, *Wow, wouldn't it be great to have a big cool drink of lemonade right now?* Suddenly a lemon tree appears right next to you and you pull down two lemons. Grab the lemons with your hands. Rest your hands on your legs, palms up facing the ceiling. Pretend you have one lemon in each of your hands. When I say go, I want you to make each of your hands into fists and squeeze your fists as hard as you can.

Imagine that you have a lemon in each of your hands and that you're squeezing the lemons to make yourself some lemonade. As you hold your fists tight, picture the fresh lemon juice filling up a tall glass. Really squeeze your fists together. You start to see the lemon juice fill up the glass just a bit. Hold it! And relax. Drop the lemons and notice how good it feels to have your hands relax after they felt so tense. It feels nice and warm and tingly to have your hands relaxed.

But you're really thirsty, so tighten your fists again. Squeeze them as hard as you can. Ready...go! Hold your fists for the count of three. One...two...three. Squeeze really hard. And relax. Drop the lemons. You've filled up your glass halfway now. Phew!

Notice how your muscles and your hands relax, and how great it feels. And again, squeeze the lemons. Hold them as tight as you can for the count of three. Ready, go...one...two...three. Excellent! You did it! You filled up your glass with lemonade.

Okay, relax. Drop the lemons. Ahhhh. You take a drink, your thirst is quenched, and you feel so proud of yourself.

The Turtle and the Stream

Now pretend you are a little turtle sitting on a rock in a beautiful stream. You hear the water of the stream rushing around you. The sun is on your face. The birds are singing overhead and you feel happy and content. You take a deep breath in, and out, as the sun warms your face. All of a sudden, you hear the sound of something falling into the water. And you decide to tuck your head into your shell.

When I say go, pretend that you're tucking your head in your turtle shell by lifting your shoulders up toward your ears. Pretend you are hiding your head in your shell. Ready? Go! Lift your shoulders to your ears and hide your head in your shell. Hold it! One...two...three...feel the tightness in your shoulders as you lift them to your ears. And relax.

Drop your shoulders. You realize that the sound you heard was just the sound of a little fish splashing in the stream. Ahhh. Notice how great it feels to have your shoulders nice and relaxed. Take a deep breath, in and out. You feel so happy. You continue to enjoy the sunny day.

But uh-oh, there's another, bigger splashing sound in the stream. You decide to tuck your head back in your shell. So raise your shoulders to your ears. Excellent! Hold them...one... two...three. Hold them really tight. And phew, relax. Drop your shoulders. You see that the sound you heard was just the sound of a little duck landing in the water. You listen to him quacking and you realize that you are very safe. You can relax your shoulders again. Notice how nice it feels to have your shoulders so relaxed.

And once again you hear another sound in the stream. You

tuck your head back in your turtle shell and you hold it for the count of three. Ready? One…two…three…hold it. And relax. Notice the difference between having your shoulders tense and your shoulders relaxed. You laugh to yourself as you realize that the sound you heard was just a frog jumping off a rock to take a swim. You feel nice and warm and relaxed, and you decide to take a swim too.

Splash!

Relax Your Face

You are sitting down and you are drinking your nice glass of lemonade. You take a deep breath, in and out, feeling your breath hit the back of your throat. You feel happy and peaceful. All of your worries have left your mind and you enjoy feeling the cool breeze on your face. All of a sudden, you begin to hear the buzzing of a little friendly fly circling around you. It is looking for a place to rest because it has been flying around all day in the hot sun.

Suddenly you see that the fly has landed right on your nose. That silly little fly! Your hands are holding your glass of lemonade, so you try to scrunch up your nose and tighten your face to see if the fly will leave. Ready? Scrunch up your face and nose really tight. Hold it…one…two…three. And relax. Ahh. That little fly seems to have flown away. Aren't you glad you don't have to keep your face scrunched up all day long? You take another sip of cool lemonade and take another deep breath.

Suddenly the fly comes back and lands on your forehead. Scrunch up your face, nose, and forehead really tight, and maybe the fly will go away. Ready? One…two…three…hold it. Feel how tight it is. And relax. Your face is nice and relaxed, and the fly takes off.

Oh, here he comes again. He lands on your nose. One more time, scrunch up your face really tight. Feel the muscles in your face as you scrunch it up. Hold it for the count of three. One…two…

three. And relax. The fly takes off, and you see him fly far away. You laugh when you realize how much he liked resting on your face.

Hungry at the Beach

You are lying in the sand at the beach, on your favorite beach towel. You feel nice and relaxed. You are taking deep breaths, feeling your lungs fill up with air, just like two balloons. All of a sudden you decide that you are feeling hungry. You can smell delicious food being cooked at the snack stand nearby.

You see a shortcut to the snack stand. There's a very narrow passage between two big trees, and that path leads right to the food. You decide to go. You have to hold in your stomach muscles really tight in order to fit between the two trees. When I say go, hold your stomach muscles in really tight. Ready? Go. One...two...three. And relax. You did it, you just made it between the two trees.

You're about to get something to eat when you realize you've left your money on the beach towel. Once again, you have to hurry and slip between the two trees to get back to your beach towel. Ready? Hold your stomach in really tight and pretend you are slipping between the two trees. One...two...three. And relax. Phew. You've got your money now. You can slip through the narrow passage again to get your snack. Ready? Once again, hold your stomach muscles in really tight. One...two...three. And relax. Notice how great it feels to have your stomach muscles relaxed. Picture yourself getting your favorite snack and eating it at the snack stand. You feel great.

Taking a Nap

Imagine that you are a cute little puppy cuddled up on a blanket on a cold winter's day. You can hear the sound of the wind and the snow outside your window. You are snuggled up on a blanket next to your brother and sister puppies. You feel so relaxed that you decide to take a quick nap.

You breathe in and out and you feel so relaxed that you fall asleep in front of the fireplace, listening to the crackling flames as you sleep. You feel so safe and warm. Nothing in the world can harm you. You are very comfortable and happy.

Now you are waking up from your nap. You decide to stretch your paws out in front of you. Pretend you are stretching your paws by reaching both of your arms out in front of you. You are stretching your arms and you feel the pulling at your shoulders as you stretch. Ready? Stretch your arms out in front of you. One... two... three. And relax. Drop your arms to your side. Ahhh. It feels so great to stretch after a nap.

Let's try it again. Ready? Stretch. One... two... three... hold it. And relax. Drop your arms to the side. You feel such a difference between tight muscles and relaxed muscles. It makes you feel so happy to see just how relaxed you can be. And once again, let's give it one more stretch. Ready? Stretch your arms out in front of you. One... two... three... hold it. Feel the pulling at your shoulders. And relax. Let your arms drop to your sides. Wow, what a good stretch you had after your nap. All of the other puppies start to wake up too. A few of them take a stretch as well, as their eyes are feeling very sleepy.

The Strong, Tall Tree

Pretend you are a tall tree standing in the middle of a field of grass and flowers. You are standing tall, feeling so strong and powerful, there is nothing in the world that is more capable than you. You are putting all of your energy into feeling strong, brave, and tall.

Suddenly a light wind begins to blow gently. You feel your branches sway slightly. The wind gets a little stronger. In order to make sure you stay brave and strong, tense up your whole body and hold it tense to the count of three. Tighten your fists, your feet, your stomach, your shoulders, your face, all together. Ready? Go. One...two...three...hold it. Notice how tense you feel all over. And relax.

Taking a deep breath, in and out, notice how great it feels to be nice and relaxed, and to feel your limbs drop to your side. The wind dies down for a while, and you take a few deep breaths in. You are glad you can tense up your limbs and your branches, so that all of them stay strong in the wind.

Oh, here it comes again, there's another burst of wind. Tense up your branches. Tense up your arms and legs and feet and stomach. If you tense up your body, then the wind won't break any branches. Excellent. One...two...three. And relax. Notice how great it feels to have your body relaxed rather than tensed. Take a deep breath in and out, and notice how wonderful it feels to be relaxed rather than tense.

And one more time. Tense up your body. Hold it...one...two...three. And relax. Ahh. The wind is slowing down now, and you feel just a gentle breeze on your face. You feel happy and calm. Pretend that the leaves of your tree are gently blowing in the calm breeze.

I Can Relax!

You have just done an excellent job of tensing and relaxing your muscles. Notice how calm you feel as your muscles are relaxed and your mind is clear. If a worry thought comes into your mind, gently tell it to go away and refocus your thoughts on your breathing and your feelings of relaxation. Using these skills, you can help to relax yourself anywhere you are. You can tense and relax each muscle group until you're feeling more relaxed overall. You feel so proud of yourself right now, because you did such a good job of following the instructions and relaxing.

Picture yourself in your relaxing place again. If you chose the beach, put yourself back on the beach one last time. Listen to the waves crash on the shore. If you chose another relaxing place, imagine again the sounds you hear. You feel relaxed and proud as you breathe in. You feel you can do anything and accomplish anything you want. You are surrounded by people who love you and care about you. Your confidence and happiness grow as you see how you can make yourself relax.

Take a deep breath in and out, and enjoy feeling relaxed.

Let's get ready to finish now. First, I'm going to count down from five to one. Each time I say a number, I'd like you to take a deep breath in and out, thinking "relax" each time you breathe out. Ready? Five... breathe in, out, relax. You're doing great.

Four... breathe in, out, relax. You're feeling more relaxed now.

Three... breathe in, out, relax. Feel your mind clear.

Two... breathe in, out, relax. You feel so good about what you just did.

One... breathe in, out, relax. Great.

Now I want you to gradually open your eyes. You are feeling so refreshed as you open your eyes. You feel so good about yourself as your eyes open wider and wider. You've done an amazing job. As you become more awake, you realize that you can have this relaxed feeling whenever you want it, whether it is before a test, before bedtime, when you are nervous, or any other time you want. You can practice feeling more relaxed by doing the exercises you just learned. Every time you practice, you get better and better at relaxing.

You did a great job today.

*   *   *

Implementing the strategies I've outlined in this chapter will be most helpful if your child tends to be highly frightened by the physical sensations often associated with anxiety. He will gain a better understanding of what's happening in his body and how to control his fears. And through progressive muscle relaxation (especially if he practices the skill regularly), he will learn how to reduce feelings of tension, easing his body and his mind.

CHAPTER 9

Changing Avoidant Behaviors

The Power of Parental Reinforcement

Anxious children typically contend with situations they find tough by relying on avoidant behaviors.

We recognize what is called "overt avoidance," just *not doing* or *not going* (to the birthday party, the ballet class, the school presentation). Some children engage in more subtle forms of avoidance; they grit their teeth at the difficulty, all the while telling themselves, "Relax, relax, relax," or distracting themselves by thinking of something else, essentially pretending they're not there. That's a tactic that may enable a youngster to endure the momentary stress, but it doesn't promote true bravery.

Exactly how a child manages to avoid doing the thing that makes him anxious or confronting the situation he fears can take many forms, and in the previous chapters I've described a number of common scenarios:

• The boy who believes nothing he does is good enough destroys his Lego construction and flings the blocks across the floor in a fit of frustration. He sits in the corner and refuses to play anymore.

• The girl who has a hard time joining the other kids at preschool stays pasted to her mother, weeping silently.

• Worried about his performance in class and not knowing the answers, a child acts up, disrupting the day's activities and bothering the other kids. Or he says he feels sick and he wants to go to the nurse's office.

• Nervous about leaving for school, a child refuses to get dressed or delays so long that she misses the bus or arrives late.

• He's afraid of dogs and runs off crying at the sight of one.

• A child is afraid her mother will forget to pick her up and asks for endless reassurances that mom will return.

Avoidant children also often cling to their safety behaviors and objects—an activity to perform every night, a lucky "something" that they are convinced will keep trouble away:

• One boy won't leave home without a certain water bottle and mints his mother gave him to settle his tummy.

• One girl believes that as long as she's wearing blue—even just a scarf, socks, or gloves—she'll be okay.

These coping strategies do not lead to success. In fact, they only strengthen worry thoughts and the fear of normal physical sensations, keeping the cycle of anxiety alive. One key tactic in helping your child change avoidant behaviors is to pay very little attention to them.

Decreasing the Negative, Increasing the Positive

"Reinforcement" suggests something good and hoped for. You reinforce a sagging fence so it won't fall down. The ball club sends in reinforcements when the team needs support. In psychology, the term is attached to behavior: Any behavior that is paid attention to will increase; any behavior that is not paid attention to will decrease. It's easy to see, then, that parental reinforcement—where and how we pay attention—has the potential to produce good and hoped-for results or not-so-good and undesirable results.

If you are giving a lot of attention to your child's anxious behaviors, you are reinforcing anxiety. Attention, also, comes in various forms:

• Mom immediately tells the boy who's throwing his Lego blocks around and having a fit that he's really doing well, everything he's built looks wonderful.

• Dad reassures the girl who's fearful about going on the playdate or to the birthday party that she can call anytime and they'll pick her up and bring her home.

• The boy who's making a fuss in the classroom because he's axious is told by the teacher to sit out (what he was secretly wanting to do). Or he goes to the nurse's office and she comforts him and calls his parent, suggesting the boy should probably stay home until he's feeling better.

• The kid who bombards his parents with worry thoughts is told not to worry, everything's fine.

• Mom gives attention to anxious or oppositional behavior by reacting in frustration and anger and doling out a punishment (another kind of reinforcement).

How reinforcement of avoidance can take hold—and why it's so tempting to offer and so difficult to stop—is illustrated by one family's experiences.

Avery, a 10-year-old, required her father to go through a

particular ritual every evening at her bedtime. She believed that if he did not do this, bad things would happen the following day to her or to the family. It started on a fairly small scale: dad should give her a kiss, spin around once, give her another kiss, and say that he loved her. The routine became more elaborate. At the time I saw the family, every night when Avery got into bed, this father gave her a kiss, spun around, jumped in place five times, spun around again, gave her a hug, shouted "I love you I love you I love you" three times, and gave her another kiss. Dad was like a puppet on a string, doing everything his daughter demanded.

His explanation: "I do it because it works. It just takes a couple of minutes. It's the fastest way to quiet her down and get her to go to sleep. If I don't do this stuff, she cries and calls out and keeps her sisters awake. I do it because I'm tired and I want to relax after a long day and go to bed myself. I do it to give myself a break!"

That's a pretty good summary of the rationale for many of our responses to our children's anxious behaviors. We say the soothing words, offer the excessive reassurances, give in to the avoidance or the compulsive needs, because it works. For the moment. Maybe we're tired and there's a lot else going on and we just wish to keep the peace. Maybe we get caught up in all the heightened emotion our child is exhibiting. And of course we want to alleviate a child's distress and unhappiness.

We helped Avery come to see that her thoughts were not fused with people's actions, and that just because she thinks a bad thing will occur doesn't mean it will. We were able to test-drive the hypothesis that even when her father didn't carry out the bedtime performance, everyone was still alive and well the next day. We built in rewards. Avery got a lot of praise in the morning for successfully dealing with her worry thoughts. But it took awhile to get there, and the harder part was encouraging dad to cease and desist the established routine.

He had a tough time with it. There was to be no jumping, no spinning, no shouting, but for several nights, he confessed, he still performed his assigned actions, after Avery fussed and cried and made demands. I tried to explain that in the short run the change would be hard to put into practice, but it was going to be best for his child in the long run. The more he acquiesced to her wishes, the more he was inadvertently sending a message that her thoughts were true, that there would be trouble ahead, and the more entrenched her anxiety became. Look to the future, I suggested; picture her in high school and in college. Do you want her to need you there, jumping around before she can get to sleep? He did not, of course. So we had to help her develop better, more resilient coping skills.

Eventually, he was onboard with the plan, and together with Avery's mom (she'd actually been rolling her eyes at the silly rituals) he figured out where to be and what to do while Avery was having her tantrum. The other kids would close their doors and put pillows over their heads to block out all the noise.

It took just two nights without dad jumping, spinning, and shouting for Avery to adapt.

So the second lesson this family's story conveys is that changing your typical responses might mean toughing it out for a while. It might mean biting the bullet and putting up with even more negative, more demanding, noisier activity. There may be protests and a few tears. But it won't last long, because kids really do want to get better.

In the following chapter, I'll describe how a child develops adaptive coping behavior, and gets over fears, through a well-researched technique known as "exposure." The strategies will require you, in many cases, to shift the focus of your parenting attention. You will be conscious of what is called "differential reinforcement," making sure that you support the brave behavior and pay less attention to the nonbrave behavior. You're not turning away from your child in distress; you won't totally ignore him, as if his unhappiness doesn't interest you. Just make sure you're paying a lot more attention to the positive stuff—through noticing when he takes a brave step, through praise. And lay it on thick.

Make a big deal of his small successes. "I can't get over how brave you're being. I can't wait to call Daddy and tell him. He's going to be so proud of you."

Make it specific. If you want to see a particular behavior increase, tell him exactly what he did that you like—the labeled praise that I described in chapter 4. That is, not just "You're such a great kid" but "I love that you put your coat on so quickly." "I love that you took such confident steps to the birthday party."

Be careful not to insert a little negative in there. I've heard parents say, "You're getting dressed so quickly. You usually don't do it that way." You don't want to slap him with the negative after you've reinforced the positive.

Tell your child ahead of time why you're going to be (largely) ignoring the nonbrave behavior and that to get your attention again he'll need to use one of his skills. "If you're complaining, crying, and making noise, I'm not going to be listening to that. But I'm going to pay a lot of attention if I see you're doing your detective thinking, because I know that's going to help you a lot."

Praise is extremely effective in increasing the positive. A reward—a concrete, physical something or other—is equally good. Very young children are thrilled to see stickers, the gold stars signifying success, building up on their accomplishment charts, or the Bravery Ladders I describe in the next chapter.

Older kids often become animatedly engaged in figuring out a "reward store" for themselves, a place that holds special treats they will earn for taking brave steps.

Modeling Positive Behaviors

If mom or dad consistently voices fears about life, it's especially challenging for the child to take on the hard task of changing his worry thoughts. If the parent overreacts with concern about her own heightened physical sensations, the child may sense that a racing heartbeat and a dizzy head are truly threatening. Just as it's important to make the effort to model more "positive thinking," it's good to be aware of our own perhaps maladaptive behaviors and make adjustments.

In some families, obsessive-compulsive disorder can affect several members. Compulsions, essentially "safety" behaviors intended to relieve the anxiety created by irrational thoughts, can be particularly hard to eliminate. One mother and son had great success through a joint approach to adopting brave behaviors.

Nine-year-old Aaron jumped into the pool at his town's community center, and his toe brushed against a girl's butt. After that, he believed that his toe was contaminated, and he wound up not wearing his sock and shoe on that foot. Aaron's mom was frustrated and embarrassed; her son was walking around like a weird kid with only one shoe.

Aaron was also washing his hands constantly, fifteen times or more a day; when I met him, they were cracked and bleeding. He found many things "icky," including his thoughts, and if something bad entered his mind he'd have to spit it out — literally spit on the floor to rid himself of the offending thought.

I limited the number of washes he was allowed and the length of time the faucet could be running. We also had him use lotion. But it became clear that at home, Aaron's mother was also a compulsive washer. She recognized this and worried that she was reinforcing her son's behavior with her own extreme reactions to anything dirty and her need to clean herself.

We developed what we called an "icky scavenger hunt," a kind of Bravery Ladder, for Aaron. His mom took part in it, too, because she did want to model more appropriate, less compulsive behavior. Each time they touched something messy, perhaps an item that was to be tossed in the garbage, they were not to wash their hands; they had to stay with the anxious feelings and see what happened. For the boy, who liked to play basketball, we made a daily scorecard: one side was the OCD team, the other side was Aaron. Every time he scrubbed after an "icky" encounter, the OCD side got a point. Every time he was able to resist, Aaron could give himself the point.

In fact, he was highly motivated to win for his team, and soon he had all the points and OCD had none. Both mother and child ended up doing extremely well with the icky scavenger hunt.

Eventually, Aaron was able to consider whether his toe was actually contaminated. We drew up another series of steps, starting with Aaron being able to put his sock on again, though it made him a little anxious. Once the sock was conquered, he put on his shoe. His OCD disappeared, including his need to spit out bad thoughts. He had stopped swimming, an activity he loved, and after our therapy he returned to the pool.

A number of years after I treated Aaron, a tall young man arrived at the clinic asking to see me. He introduced himself and said: "Dr. Pincus, you helped me when I was a little kid. We did the icky scavenger hunt. I just wanted to tell you, I'm in high school now and I'm the captain of the swim team. I thought you'd be proud."

In chapter 10, "The Bravery Ladder," you'll see how the skills (for the child and for the parent) involved in changing "what I think, what I feel, what I do" work to overcome a child's anxieties.

The Bravery Ladder

Step by Step to Success

From her earliest days, Jenny, toted along in a baby carrier, accompanied her mother and father on camping and hiking adventures. As she got older, they loved watching her discover the joys of nature, splashing in streams and catching frogs and dragonflies. They told me they were proud of their daughter, the intrepid explorer.

When Jenny was 5, she disturbed a wasps' nest on the porch of the cabin where the family was vacationing. She was stung multiple times and her frantic parents rushed to an emergency clinic. Although she recovered nicely, she quickly developed a fear of bugs that began to interfere with her life. Jenny first came to see me when she was 6.

Her mother explained that after the incident with the wasps, Jenny cowered when she saw a spider or caterpillar, and then began hiding inside for fear of encountering a bug. She did not want to leave their apartment. Though mom and dad gently encouraged her to go out, she would not. They tried promising to keep a lookout for bugs and protect her from them. It didn't work.

Jenny had also begun to refuse to play outside at recess with her first-grade class, and her teacher suggested to the parents that perhaps they should consider another school. When the girl wouldn't go to the family cabin during the summer, her parents' frustration reached a peak; they had no idea how this fearfulness had somehow grown so great that Jenny didn't want to do anything fun outdoors.

One of the first things they said to me was how much they missed their once spunky little girl, the one who was always eager to explore.

Even from the first therapy session, I was struck by how strongly Jenny was motivated to learn how to stop feeling so afraid. She knew her parents wanted to "protect" her from bugs, but she told me that she wanted to be brave on her own. I taught her how to break down anxiety into its component parts, and she proved to be very capable at identifying the anxious thoughts, feelings, and behaviors she experienced when she saw a bug.

At the end of the session, I brought Jenny's parents into the room, and asked her to tell her mom and dad what she'd learned. Jenny described the three parts of anxiety as "what I think, what I feel, and what I do." As she explained how we were going to teach her skills to break the cycle—"I am going to learn this so we can go on picnics again!"—I glimpsed the bubbly adventurer her parents had told me about.

During therapy, I encouraged Jenny to "examine the evidence" like a detective regarding whether bugs were harmful, and she decided that most were too busy to even notice her. I taught her not to catastrophize each encounter with a bug.

She was ready to take a step. We looked at a picture book about insects. My colleagues and I brought in any we could catch—flies, ladybugs, small spiders. We even had a tarantula, a pet belonging to one of my associates. Jenny did a great job of gradually approaching the bugs, first watching them inside bottles and other containers. Eventually, she was able to let a few ladybugs crawl on her hands, and she giggled when she let them walk over her father's and mother's arms. After only three two-hour sessions, these parents felt their daughter was already back on track to being the old Jenny.

Later that summer, I was thrilled to receive a letter from Jenny, complete with a photo, telling me how she had spent a summer's night at her family's cabin catching fireflies with her mom and dad.

This young child mastered her anxiety—and got brave—through exposure to the creatures she feared.

Exposure Therapy

Exposure therapy is a treatment used for helping people overcome phobias that typically involves gradually decreasing the individual's irrational fear of an object or situation. In other words, put yourself in contact with the trigger (high places, say), experience the anxiety, and then prevent your avoidant response to it (panic and going to extreme lengths to avoid ever being in a skyscraper or a glass-sided elevator).

One mother remembered her own "sheer terror" at speaking in front of a group. She traced its origins to an episode in her childhood when she was chosen to recite a poem to a small audience of parents, teachers, and other kids at her elementary school holiday party. She forgot the words. Everyone stared at her. "My mind was paralyzed," she said. "I raced off the stage before I burst into tears, and in the audience there was a smattering of laughter and clapping, which actually made me feel worse."

Her phobia about public speaking became so severe that in

her first postcollege job she was sick to her stomach before having to attend a staff meeting and panicky about even talking to coworkers casually. "In any kind of formal setting or among people I didn't know, it was a nightmare." She looked for a solution. "A therapist helped me set up a kind of slow and easy approach, first making a point of joining in a conversation that was under way, then telling myself I was going to offer one comment during the meeting, focusing my attention on the person I found least terrifying, and so on. This turned out to be extremely useful."

She was keenly sensitive to her young daughter's generalized anxiety, and was considering a treatment program that might help.

Some children do experience irrational and excessive fears of particular objects, like Jenny's reaction to bugs, moving beyond the developmentally "normal" into the "red flag" territory I described in chapter 2. For example, clowns are a big problem for many kids, possibly because the painted-on expressions don't match the displayed emotions, or possibly because of the unpredictability of the clown's actions. One youngster might "normally" shy away and not accept the lollipop that's offered; another will scream in fright, clutch his parent desperately, and not calm down until far after and far away from the situation.

In setting up exposures to a fear of clowns, we'd start by looking at drawings of clowns in a picture book. The child might color the image in a workbook. We'd have some props to handle and play with, like a stick-on red nose or a woolly wig. We might also bring in a real-live clown to say hello, and the child would learn to interact with him.

Each action is one step on that child's Bravery Ladder.

Exposure therapy is really the key way to treating many of these phobic reactions and anxiety disorders. The child is encouraged to *not* avoid the thing she's afraid of, and to approach it in a controlled way. She will experience anxiety, but as she remains in the moment, right there, it begins to lessen naturally. She becomes habituated to the feeling, and realizes that it is normal and it will not hurt her. During an exposure, she does not call on the relaxation techniques she may have been practicing. She is not telling herself, Breathe in…breathe out…deep breaths… just relax.

Although relaxation strategies can be extremely helpful, and kids love learning the skills, they actually can interfere with the process of habituation to anxious feelings that we want to take place during an exposure. It makes sense, really. If the child is urging herself to breathe deeply and relax, she is both distancing herself from the thing or situation she's afraid of and almost sending herself a message that it clearly is harmful and danger-ous, just as she suspected in her worst thoughts.

During an exposure, she will also leave at home her "safety" items — the lucky trinket, the mints for her tummy, the gloves in the good-luck color. Engaging in safety behaviors gives a child the illusion that she's all right, she's safe, but it maintains anxiety in the long run because she attributes her success to the object or behavior rather than being able to say, "I'm doing this on my own. I can handle the situation."

In gaining mastery over that thing she's afraid of, she perhaps also learns something about herself that she can apply to other situations.

In fact, in our work with anxiety disorders, we've discovered that it often isn't necessary to fully treat more than one fear. If a youngster is particularly terrified about thunderstorms, for exam-ple, when we help her control her response to thunderstorms, she begins to apply the skills she's learned to her other fears. If your child for the first time successfully and happily manages a sleepover at a classmate's house, she'll probably find it less stress-ful to leave for the next birthday party.

Kids like exposure therapy. They take to the idea of working their way up a ladder. What pleases them is that it's active, something they do; it's not just sitting in a room talking to someone about their worries.

The Bravery Ladder is the cornerstone of the process we call "Bravery-Directed Interaction."

Bravery-Directed Interaction

The CDI skills that you've become good at during five-minutes-a-day special time — using labeled praise, reflecting your child's emotions, describing what's going on — will be extremely handy as you help him gain control of his fears. If you meet with resistance and noncompliance to an agreed-upon activity, you will remember to discourage any emotionally charged interactions that can lead to bad feelings all around.

You have used the cycle of anxiety model described in chapter 6 to try to break down your youngster's difficulties into what he's thinking, feeling, and doing when he's in an anxious situation. You have a pretty good idea of what he needs to change in order to progress.

And perhaps you have introduced him to — and helped him practice — some strategies to add to his "toolbox" of coping skills: for example, relaxing his muscles or playing detective to figure out just how real his worries are. These will start to help him feel better and more confident.

In Bravery-Directed Interaction, your child will have his homework: climbing the Bravery Ladder. You will have some homework, too. Most kids truly do want to overcome their fears. But conquering the anxiety beast, even one step at a time, isn't easy. This is, again, an interactive effort. Mom or dad or both can and should be part of it in several particular ways:

- brainstorming
- rewarding
- helping motivate by creating opportunities
- promoting practicing
- meeting resistance

The Dos and Don'ts of Helping Your Child Get Brave

A few general reminders:

- DON'T give extra positive attention to your child when she's complaining or distressed about separating from you. It's okay to be caring and reflect her feelings; tell her you understand how hard it is to try to do this on her own, and you're going to be very proud of her for trying.

- DO save the extra praise for after she's begun to approach the new situation, even for taking a small step toward the larger goal. Say, "You've done a great job. I'm very proud of the way you try new things even when it's hard."

- DON'T pull your child out of tough situations because you want to avoid "making a scene."

- DO help her engage in developmentally appropriate behaviors and tell her you're confident that she can do this selected activity.

- DON'T try to make all the choices for your child.

- DO let her make small decisions on her own. Just as you practiced in CDI, it's okay to let children lead. This is a useful rule to remember when you and she are talking over a Bravery Ladder: What would she like to work on first? Going on a playdate, for example, or to a friend's birthday party?

(continued)

- DON'T worry too much if your child is slow to start. Learning to be brave takes time.
- DO encourage without nagging. Let her know that it will get easier each time she tries something new. Let her hear you brag about her to grandma or a good friend. She realizes how proud she has made you.

Building the Ladder

The Bravery Ladder is another term for exposure therapy, similar to the "Fear and Avoidance Hierarchy" widely used with adults in treating anxiety. The hierarchy—actions climbing from the least feared aspect of confronting the anxious situation up to the most feared and difficult—will be different for each person.

To introduce your child to the whole idea, you might want to adapt the explanation we use at our clinic: "We use a Bravery Ladder here to help kids practice feeling more brave and happy. Kids list different activities on the ladder. You get to decide which one you want to work on first. Next to each activity, there is a place for a sticker or a happy face. When you complete the activity, you get a special sticker on your Bravery Ladder."

Figure out the steps together with your child, but give some thought first to which item or items you would like to see him attempt and, especially, which you think will be most doable. The bottom step of the ladder is the action you feel your child can master. It should not be something so hard that he might fail at it, but don't make it so easy that it's just a joke.

He might not understand the concept of a controlled approach. Suppose you say, "Honey, I know you'd like to play soccer with the other kids, you've told me you would like to, but you have trouble joining the group. Let's think of how you can make this easier for yourself." Your child may reply, "It's okay, Mom, I'll go next week," and hope that ends the conversation. Explain further. Tell him that you don't intend to force him into anything. You do not expect him to dive right into a situation that is difficult for him. Instead, you are going to help him take one step at a time.

Especially with a young child, a parent will need to come up with a list of sensible, graduated actions. Then go over the suggestions and talk to him about which item he'd like to try first. If he's resistant to even the easiest one on the list, see if you can break it down into a couple of smaller steps.

Bravery Ladders can include eight items, ten items, or even more if you want. Ideally, each will be specific and detailed: What time of day will he be taking this step? How many minutes will it occupy or how long should he do it for? Where does it take place? Who else will be there? And so on. The top step (number 1) is the hardest; the bottom is the easiest, so your child will work his way up. Progress is noted by a sticker next to each step. One success breeds another.

When working with a child, I usually say, "Let's master the first step." Perhaps she takes the step, but not comfortably; she managed to go on a sleepover, but woke up a few times and cried. I will suggest that she try that one again. Your child may need to practice a step a few times until her anxiety comes down from, say, an 8 to a 3 on the 0-to-8 scale, before she's ready to move up. Some children have given themselves half a sticker (they actually cut it in half) because they felt they didn't make it all the way to the next step and need more practice.

We usually focus on one task at a time, but sometimes a kid says, "I think I can do two of these right now"—touching a dog, for example, and going to the dog run at the park. There's no one prescription, no rule that says "a new week, a new step." Tailor the process to your child.

Write up your Bravery Ladder. Describe each action in simple language that your youngster can understand, with a space next to it for the rewarding sticker or happy face. With an older child, you might want to just use a big check mark. Parents have sometimes questioned the sticker chart. "Does that really work in this day and age?" they have asked. "My kid has anxiety issues, but like all the other third graders we know she can also seem kind of aware and cool and she knows the names of the pop singers, and I just wonder if getting a gold star is going to make much of an impression."

I've really never seen a young child scoff at the sticker chart. It works because it reminds the child she's been successful at something that has been tough for her. And of course it comes with praise and family attention, and that's the truly encouraging part. Some children, even at quite young ages, are able to verbalize that they just want to not be afraid anymore, that the act of getting better is the biggest reward. The gold star is proof to the child that she's making progress. Tangible reinforcers like this do lose their saliency over time, but they're an effective way to kick off the process of changing behavior.

On the Bravery Ladder, draw a little picture of the action, the brave step, if necessary. Some ladders we've seen have been wonderfully colorful affairs with drawings and cut-out illustrations from magazines. One ladder (Dad was an artist) had a series of sketches across the top, showing a kid climbing a mountain — starting on the ground looking skyward, halfway up, almost there, finally standing triumphantly at the peak, smiling broadly and raising his arms in victory.

Your child's "homework" is to practice his first chosen activity from the ladder. But you don't have to *call* it homework. Talk to him about how great it will be to feel really brave in trying new things. If he complains about how all this is going to be so hard, empathize and reflect his emotions: "I know you feel this will be hard, and I am going to be so impressed when you try your first brave activity."

And there will be a reward.

Bravery Dollars and the Reward Store

One girl was experiencing a great deal of separation anxiety. When were her parents going to leave her? When would they return? What were they doing during the day? What if something bad happened to them? I helped this family design a Bravery Ladder, a bravery treasure box, and a Reward Store. Each time their child successfully took a step, or tried very hard to, she got to pick a reward from the box, which held a variety of simple treats her parents had written down on little pieces of paper— having a picnic in the living room in the winter, going to the park zoo in time to watch the seals being fed, working on a scrapbook to give to her grandfather.

These were activities the child loved. She did feel rewarded. And her parents were rewarded, too. It helped them to recognize that "We don't have to *not* reinforce our child. We're just going to shift when and how we do it, shift the attention a little." The Reward Store obviously provides a child with applause for entering into a previously avoided situation and behaving bravely. It also helps her parents continue to nurture an appropriate, positive interaction and to shape desired behavior.

In our clinic, we have the kids come up with enjoyable activities for their Reward Store list, mostly things they could do with their parents, such as the living room picnic, taking the trip to the zoo, playing Twister (dad, too) or another family game, eating dessert first, working on a special craft. Talk this over with your child and think of at least five rewards that he can earn by practicing situations on the Bravery Ladder. Write them down. Put them in a treasure box.

Your rewards don't have to include things that cost money. In fact, maybe they shouldn't. One girl who was encouraged to take brave steps and was promised a reward said, "Okay, I'll do it, but I think what would really help me is if I got the Kate Spade messenger bag. That would do it for me." Her parents bought the bag. And, maybe not too surprisingly, it didn't do it for her.

With young children, one technique that often works like a charm is the creation of Bravery Dollars.

In our clinic session, the child and I will make a paper design that looks like a dollar bill. He can draw a little face in the middle, color the bill if he wants to, or copy it onto green paper. Some kids make a photocopy of their face, cut it out, and paste it in the center. We write BRAVERY DOLLAR at the top. We photocopy it and come up with a whole stack of bills. The child is given an inexpensive wallet, a special place for his Bravery Dollars.

Mom holds on to the Bravery Dollars. Every time she catches her child using a skill—restructuring a worry thought, for example—or taking a brave action, she gives him a dollar, or more than one. And the important point again is the process; even if he was struggling and didn't quite work through his fear, he can be rewarded for trying.

Accumulating a certain number of Bravery Dollars equals something from the Reward Store. It's a way to make this kind of reinforcement a little more fun and creative, and also to engage the child in "rating" his brave efforts. When I'm working with a child, together we figure out three levels—top rewards (maybe having a playdate with a friend at the arcade or another special activity that would be worth a lot of Bravery Dollars, after he has accomplished three steps on his ladder), medium rewards, and lower rewards. Many kids are charmingly realistic about the whole matter. "No, that's a really big reward," the child will say. "I think I have to do something bigger to get that."

Rewarding: Keeping It Fresh and Keeping It Real

Bravery Dollars and the Reward Store are popular strategies with children and not difficult for parents to execute. But to be effective, it's important to keep several behavioral principles in mind:

• *Set up guidelines.* Talk over with your child just what she needs to do to gain a particular reward. I have sometimes seen a parent produce a list of treats, but there's no clear understanding of the when and why behind them. So the child might accomplish one step on her ladder and say, "Okay, can I have this thing on my list now?" And mom says, "No, you stayed at the party for only half an hour. You have to do more than that." The parent-child interaction turns negative.

• *Have the reward equal the activity.* A small brave move or attempt earns a small reward; there's a bigger one for the most difficult steps.

• *Reward immediately.* Let the reinforcement come as soon as possible after the brave behavior or attempt. Of course, life gets frenzied; it's not always practical to reward on the spot. But I have often heard a parent say to her child, "Wonderful, we'll go to that ice cream place next Saturday. You've earned that." I've had kids say, "I did three brave things and then I was supposed to have a sleepover at my cousin's, but stuff came up and Mom never arranged it."

The child just loses steam. And kids learn quickly not to trust their parents when they don't follow through as promised. Parents tell me, "I didn't think this was so important. I thought if we did it next month, that would be fine." It is important. Capitalize on the brave momentum. Do the ice cream treat or the sleepover

(continued)

right away. Reorganize life a little to make it happen. The closer the reward is to the good behavior, the stronger its effect.

- *Make the connection clear.* Say "Wonderful, we're going to get ice cream because you did such a good job on your Bravery Ladder. You got yourself dressed and ready to leave for school without me reminding you even once. I'm proud of you, and you get a reward."

- *Create some equity in the household.* Your other child (or children) needs appreciation. Sometimes the other child decides to become a bit "unbrave," seeing his sibling getting treats. Or he becomes resentful. You might want to explain, "Janie is getting this reward for her brave behavior," and perhaps make up a little chart for all to see the positive changes that have taken place. Janie checks off how she picked up her clothes, or slept without the light on, or whatever the accomplishment. Then do something nice just for the other kid. Maybe he can get his own "brave things I do" chart.

Creating Opportunities

It helps enormously on the road to success to see yourself, the parent, as an active participant in this treatment. Your child will do his homework, taking the steps. But kids can't arrange matters all by themselves. They can't get there on their own.

Don't just wait for exposure opportunities to come up; make them happen.

One child, 7-year-old Jake, was terrified of dogs. In therapy, he and I went out to dog-walking parks and practiced a slow approach to a tiny dog. We were working up to a point at which a dog could actually jump on Jake's knee, and Jake would be able to handle that without screaming. But over time, his anxiety was not noticeably decreasing. It became clear that during all the days

Jake was not at a clinic session, he never saw a dog. Or if he did see one, he ran back inside his house or in the other direction.

I explained to his parents that if they created an opportunity during the week for a dog encounter or two, all the better. Dogs were not going to come knocking on their door to be petted. Could they visit a neighbor who owned a dog? Was there a pet store somewhere in the vicinity that they could make a point of stopping by to look at the puppies in the window?

Whatever your child's anxiety trigger, create the possibility for exposure. Set up the sleepovers. Arrange the playdates. And don't forget to follow through on the reward when she tries to take a step.

Meeting Resistance

What do you do if your child panics in a planned situation and says, "I want to leave. I don't want to do this"? How do you gently encourage him to stay? Or is it okay to leave?

Usually, we recommend waiting—sticking it out—until the child's anxiety has come down to at least half of what it was: he's visibly calmer, he's not crying. This could be for five minutes, ten minutes, or one minute. Then with labeled praise, maximize that accomplishment as being a successful step. He may still need to practice it several more times before he's ready to move on.

If you are onboard with the bravery plan while your child is resistant, sometimes tangible reinforcers—stickers, small treats, used heavily in the beginning—can work to help him feel more game to the idea.

Or figure out how to ease the pressure a little. Your child says she can't do the next step. She's kind of stuck on her Bravery Ladder, in the middle of an exposure process. Can you rearrange the circumstances to make them less stressful? One child just could not manage a sleepover at a friend's house. We brainstormed and decided that setting up a night at grandma's would make it easier; it was still a sleepover, she would still be away from her mother, it might feel a little strange, but this was doable. Another child, a teenager who had battled a fear of being alone, was freshly nervous about going away to college. She wound up staying one night in a hotel with a friend, both girls in separate rooms, and she was buoyed by her success in this small way.

But a critical principle of cognitive behavioral treatment is that the patient must be motivated. Most kids say they do want to climb a Bravery Ladder, they want to be happier, they want to get rid of their fears. Some, however, do not, or at least not to the degree that they're willing to work at it. One boy was fearful of getting sick and also terribly afraid of heights. In my office, he was shaking badly, couldn't look out the window, and was desperate to get away. His parents were having trouble bringing him into various situations, because he didn't want to try. He might attempt one small action, but then avoided and refused anything further.

If a child's resistance is seemingly intractable, I always have to wonder what else is going on. Why is this child not motivated to get better?

If this is the situation you are facing, give some thought to what the resistance is about. Sometimes for kids, getting better means they have to do things that are not only hard but will be a whole lot less fun than *not* doing them: *I have to go back to school. If I stay home, I can play my Wii, I can play games online, and that's way more reinforcing to me than going to school.*

Or: *If I show mom that I'm getting better, I won't get so much attention.*

Sometimes it's the parent who's resisting. One girl wanted to get over her crippling panic attacks. Her mother, admirably insightful about the dynamic between them, said, "You know what? If she gets totally better, I'm not going to get to go shopping with her because she's not going to want to hang out with me anymore. She's a teenager. Even if she has panic, I consider myself lucky because at least she wants to spend time with me." Her daughter was picking up on that. Mom realized she had to adjust her own thoughts and feelings.

Another girl believed that if she conquered her nighttime anxieties and stopped sleeping in her parents' bed with them, they would get divorced. Mother and father were not doing well together, there was a great deal of fighting between them, but when the child was fearful, all their attention shifted to her. She was afraid that if she got better, there'd be nothing there. Her home would be finished.

Usually, any kind of behavior has a function. Sometimes parents need to figure out the function of a child's resistant behavior. What might your child be gaining by staying afraid? What is going on in the family structure that might be sustaining your child's fear, reinforcing the anxiety? Such a critical self-analysis is a tough challenge for any parent, but it could be the key to freeing a child.

Taking the Temperature of Anxiety

During an exposure practice, the child needs to stick with it for a certain amount of time. Staying in a scary situation almost always makes it become less scary. But a child's instinct may be to leave immediately, just when her anxiety is at its peak: *Okay, I petted the dog once, I did it, now let me out of here!* Rushing from the scene, however, does not result in a successful exposure or habituation. When she leaves in a state of intense fear, she attaches that

(continued)

feeling to the situation or object. So she's back at square one the next time she sees a dog.

I explain to a child the importance of staying in the moment until her body comes down from a heightened level of anxiety, to at least half the intensity. We'll use a "fear thermometer," a sketch that represents how afraid she feels, from not at all, to a little bit, some, a lot, and very, very much.

I'll sometimes draw faces to illustrate, or cut pictures of faces from magazines. The face at 8, the highest level, is freaking out. The face at 0 is calm and smiling. Midway through, at 4, the child is feeling a little nervous and not terribly happy about things, but she can ride out the situation.

It's helpful to engage your child at a quiet time in a discussion about being afraid. Give her a way to anchor what the levels feel like by asking her to remember a time when she felt at the top, most anxious. Maybe that was in anticipation of a test in school or an athletic competition? Remember a time she was somewhere in the middle. Ask her what her body felt like at an 8 and a 5 and a 2. Remind her that when she takes a difficult step on her Bravery Ladder, her goal is to stay with it until her anxiety comes down — maybe from "a lot" to "some."

The bigger goal here is for your child to leave the difficult situation with a sense of mastery, some feelings of self-efficacy. She realizes that next time she's petting a dog, it's going to be even easier.

Promoting Practicing

A teenage boy had been doing a Bravery Ladder and making good strides in controlling his panic attacks. Then he took a kind of hiatus over a long summer. His mother explained to me at one point that they hadn't practiced recently, but that after her son did further work on his steps, they'd bring him in for a session at the clinic. In September, the boy did arrive for an appointment, and he was clearly not in good shape—shaking, distracted, and upset in my office. It seemed his progress had not only stalled, but he'd gone backward.

Part of his difficulty involved the interaction between his real wish to get better and the developmental demands of his age. A teenager, he wanted to be independent, but another part of him was crying for his mother when he was panicking. His mom said, "I blame myself. You reminded us to practice, make sure that we maximized his gains, and I didn't push and remind him enough. I let it go. I was hoping all this would just go away."

Create continuing practice opportunities for your child. Find the neighbor who has a dog your afraid-of-dogs youngster can visit, in a nice, safe, friendly setting. If your child has "eat dinner at my friend's house with her family" as a step on her Bravery Ladder, don't let the effort fade away after one success. Make some more phone calls to set up another dinner outing. Remind her that if she practices facing fears, that's how she can make them go away.

In chapter 7, I described 11-year-old Andrea, who, panicky whenever her mom or dad was a few minutes late picking her up after school or a planned activity, immediately imagined they'd been killed in a car crash. After she and I had worked on her thought-changing skills and developed bravery steps, we engineered a practice test. Andrea was told that at some unspecified time in the following week her mother would arrive ten or fifteen minutes later than scheduled. Andrea would refocus her worry thoughts and use her coping skills, and tell herself that being late didn't mean something bad happened. The girl handled the challenge just fine, and felt quite proud of herself.

Even if it does "go away," even if he's no longer so fearful, the child should keep at it. We recommend what we call "relapse prevention." He has successfully climbed the ladder, his anxiety seems to have disappeared, but it's useful, knowing he was once vulnerable, to continue to practice being brave. One child was afraid of escalators. Together, we rode on many escalators, finally successfully; she was about to enter college, and happy that she could go to a mall or department store and take the moving stairs calmly. But sometimes, she said, she experienced a little twinge of her old anxiety. I suggested that occasionally she purposefully hunt up a place with an escalator and ride it a few times. Continue practicing.

I say this a lot to my patients who are afraid of flying. Schedule a little plane jaunt to a nearby city. Just go online, find a flight to anywhere that isn't too expensive, and go.

Otherwise, confidence can wane. Fear can start to creep back.

Remember to praise your child all along the way. In our clinic, we'll go even further. We'll have a party. At the end of this chapter, I'll share a story about one brave little girl, and how all who loved and admired her gathered for a grand celebration.

Some Bravery Ladders

The ladders that follow are designed around common separation-anxiety situations and several other anxiety disorders. They are just samples, to offer you suggestions.

Your child might experience more than one of these difficulties—going on a playdate and sleeping in his own room, for example. Anxieties often cluster together, so bear that in mind as you think about the most useful ladder in your situation.

I've included the stories of several children and families I have treated that illustrate so well the interactive nature of these efforts. It's a joint venture. And often these moms and dads end up feeling just wonderful about what's happened, closer to their child and more confident in themselves as parents.

Here's the most important point: Never force your child, though a little nudging might be helpful at times. He should attempt his Bravery Ladder when he's ready. The whole goal is to develop self-efficacy, seeing himself gradually doing better.

The Child Who Hates Leaving for School

This is a classic situation for anxious kids, and one that typically drives parents crazy. After all, your child doesn't *have* to go to a birthday party. He *does* have to go to school, and mornings with an avoidant child, when everyone else in the household must get out the door, too, are both chaotic and stressful.

Before using a Bravery Ladder, take these steps to set your child up for success:

- Be sure he has a consistent bedtime.
- Be sure he eats some breakfast.
- Establish a regular morning routine and talk it over with him in a calm and matter-of-fact manner. Post the routine in a logical place, where he can see it. Either write out the tasks or, if your youngster can't yet read, draw a picture of what will be going on and what he needs to get done: a cereal bowl, a toothbrush, clothes, shoes, a backpack, the bus, and so on.

The Bravery Ladder

1. [Hardest] I left for school on time with everything in my backpack without any reminders, and I entered the school building all by myself with no fussing. I changed my worry thoughts and noticed that I can still go to school even when I am anxious about it.

2. I did number 3 on the ladder and I got to school on time.

3. I did number 4, but this time I got on the bus/in the car and walked into school with a friend, not with my parents.

4. I accomplished all of the things on my morning routine with no reminders and no fighting or resisting, and I got into the bus/car with mom/dad accompanying me.

5. I accomplished three of the things on my morning routine with one or no reminders and got into the car without any fussing or fighting.

6. I was able to change my worry thoughts when I felt anxious this morning and then did two of the things on my morning routine with only one reminder.

7. I woke up on time and also did two of the things on my morning routine with only one reminder from my parents.

8. [Easiest] I woke up on time this morning.

The Child Who's Miserable about Going on Playdates or Sleepovers

Playdates were a problem for 7-year-old Lexie, who demonstrated severe separation anxiety. During the roughly four years she'd been in preschool and grade school, her mom said, the girl rarely wanted to have a friend over to her house in the afternoon or on the weekend. When a friend did come over, Lexie always insisted her mother stay right within view. The playdates didn't last long in any case.

Lexie would not go to anyone else's house, and this was creating social and logistical difficulties for her mother. "It's become embarrassing," she said, "because I've gotten to know most of the other parents in my daughter's school, and I have to turn them down when they invite Lexie to come and play. I don't know how to explain it; it sounds like a rejection of their child. Plus, I'd like to have, say, a Saturday afternoon free to run some errands and leave her at another kid's house for a couple of hours. I can't do that."

With her daughter about to enter second grade, Lexie's mom talked to her about a Bravery Ladder, and together they came up with a number of ideas about what to include. The girl did want to try. She wanted to feel better.

The Bravery Ladder

1. [Hardest] I went on a sleepover at a friend's house who lives over five miles away and I had fun!

2. I went on a sleepover at a friend's house who lives down the block from me and had fun!

3. I went on a sleepover at my grandma's/cousin's house.

4. I had a "late playdate" from 6:00 to 8:00 at night with a friend at her house and stayed for two hours by myself.

5. I had a playdate with a friend for one hour during the day and stayed the whole time by myself.

6. I had a playdate with a friend for one hour during the day, and mom stayed at the friend's house for the first fifteen minutes.

7. I had a playdate with a friend at her house for thirty minutes, and my mom stayed for the first fifteen minutes.

8. [Easiest] I had a playdate with a friend at my house for thirty minutes and I had fun!

The Child Who Can't Go to Sleep in His Own Bed

A wonderful success story around sleeping problems involved Lucas, a 9-year-old, and his father, a busy executive who wasn't home a lot. He said to me, "I don't spend a lot of time with the kids. That's my wife's thing. I'm putting food on the table." Dad was out the door early in the morning and back late at night.

Lucas was a sad boy. He missed his father and was having great difficulties over the nighttime routine. He couldn't get to sleep and was always tired. We did finally persuade dad to come to the clinic for one teach session and discussed CDI. He was skeptical, but he said he'd give it a shot.

Lucas's parents set his bedtime for fifteen minutes later, and his father made an effort to get home a little earlier on a regular basis, so the two had time together. Just knowing that his dad wanted to be with him was huge for the boy. It was huge for his father too, who said they actually had fun talking about sports teams while they played. Lucas enjoyed it so much, and that was tremendously reinforcing for his father. Dad said, "I realized I never spent five minutes with my kid without kind of going at him about homework and stuff."

Bedtime was a sticking point. Lucas's parents were initially telling him, "This is nuts. Everybody goes to sleep. You want a pat on the back for falling asleep?" and so on. But we developed a ladder for the child, eventually having all lights off and going to bed within fifteen minutes of being told. And dad got onboard with that plan, too.

We decided that having a brave night meant completing five of the steps on his Bravery Ladder. When Lucas clocked ten brave nights in a row, we were going to have a pizza party. But best of all, his father told him, "If you have a brave night, and I think you can do it, I want you to call me and I don't care where I am, I'm going to say right out loud with you, 'Brave night! Brave night!'" As it happened, dad was at a client meeting early one morning when Lucas called, and true to his word, he shouted, "Brave night! Yeah!" On the other end of the phone, Lucas was saying it, too. Another time, the father was driving in his car when he got the call, and with the windows open he started shouting, "Brave night! Yeah!"

The child was so motivated by his dad's resounding approval that he kept up the good work. At the end of therapy, Lucas's dad took the day off and surprised Lucas with tickets to a Red Sox game—on a regular school and work day. A father-son celebration. Within a couple of weeks, Lucas was sleeping well consistently.

His father said he realized he was much happier himself, learning how to get on the floor and play with his son, simply enjoying him more. He had tears in his eyes telling me about the "Brave night!" shout-out in his car.

It wasn't necessary to teach this child other specific cognitive behavioral coping skills. The main component for success was the changed parent-child dynamic.

Before figuring out brave steps around this anxiety, here are a few tips and issues to consider:

• At your child's regular checkup with the pediatrician, ask the doctor to rule out any medical or breathing issues that could be interfering with his sleep.

• Use the rules of good sleep hygiene and practice them daily prior to starting the steps. Chapter 5 outlined ideas on what constitutes good sleep hygiene, and why it's so important in combating anxiety disorders.

• Are there particular stressors that have been occurring recently in your family or your child's life that could be interfering with his sleep? Talk with him about troublesome issues during the day so that he can clear his mind before nighttime.

• Kids can help themselves enormously by practicing simple skills to get back to sleep if they wake up. Be sure your child knows about thought-changing tools (chapter 7) and relaxation strategies (chapters 5 and 8).

Here's a sample Bravery Ladder.

The Bravery Ladder

1. [Hardest] I slept in my bed all by myself with all sources of light off! I stayed asleep all night!
2. I slept in my bed all by myself with all sources of light turned off, and if I woke up at all at night I knew how to get myself back to sleep by using my nighttime bravery skills.
3. I fell asleep by myself in my own room. Instead of using the night-light in my room, I left a little night-light on in the hallway.
4. I fell asleep by myself in my own room and didn't wake up, but I used my night-light.
5. I fell asleep by myself in my own room and didn't wake up mom/dad at all! I used my night-light and my nighttime bravery skills when I woke up.
6. I slept in my room without my sibling and fell asleep by myself. I woke up mom/dad only one time in the middle of the night and returned to my bed.
7. I slept in my room with my sibling, woke up mom/dad only one time in the middle of the night, and I returned to my bed.
8. [Easiest] I took my bed/pillow out of mom/dad's room and moved it closer to the door of their room and slept there without waking mom/dad.

The Child Who's Terrified about Entering Social Situations

Social phobia, in which a child experiences great anxiety over interactions with people, is an especially disruptive disorder. I have often worked with children who have a shy temperament and who, by the middle years of childhood, have simply failed to pick up good social skills. They may know what these skills are, but their inhibition has become so pervasive and entrenched that they're paralyzed with anxiety in social encounters.

One boy, 10-year-old Will, came for therapy because his mother was concerned about his lack of friends. "He never gets together with other kids," she said. "I think he's been pretty much rejected by his peers." Will was keenly interested in a summer "space camp" that was coming up, but terrified about going and being around new people.

He and I spent some time role-playing. We practiced initiating a conversation. Kids want to talk about what they like, Will thought, so he'd give that a try.

Will asked me questions to begin. "What's your favorite movie?" he asked. "Well, I really love *The Wizard of Oz*," I replied, "I've probably seen it five times." Will stared at me. Silence. "So, what's your favorite food?" he said. "Pizza, definitely," I answered. More staring and silence. Like many children who have trouble talking to others, Will had no idea how to keep a conversation going. We discussed how important it is to try, very hard, to attend to what the other fellow is saying and respond to that, and to try to ignore one's own worries. Will decided he could say, "Really? Why do you like *The Wizard of Oz* so much?" "Do you like pizza with just the cheese? I like it with sausage and other stuff." That was a start.

Work with your child to increase his repertoire of social skills, so he'll feel he knows how to interact with the world a bit more competently. As was true for Will, making eye contact—just looking at the person he's talking to with a relaxed face—can be tough for kids with social phobia. Voice quality might need improvement. Some children talk so softly or tentatively that no one can hear them. Kids can also learn that body language conveys an impression: either *I'm enjoying talking to you* or *I wish I were anywhere else right now.*

Parents often do extremely well role-playing with a socially inhibited youngster, getting into a conversation about favorite movies or food or hockey or any topic that will interest the child or has something to do with his life. Could he benefit from practicing how to call someone on the phone? Or how to apologize if he unintentionally offended a classmate? Or how to ask to join a group that's already engaged in a game or activity? Focusing on one skill at a time is useful.

Children like Will who gather tips about initiating and maintaining conversation usually meet with some degree of success pretty quickly. The environment provides them with reinforcement: somebody smiles back; they feel emboldened.

Here's the Bravery Ladder Will set up for himself.

The Bravery Ladder

1. [Hardest] I went to space camp for a week this summer!
2. I went to a new painting class with kids my age for an hour one Saturday morning.
3. I went to the lunchroom and sat at a table with some kids I didn't know and joined a conversation.
4. I went to an after-school club by myself and talked with a kid I knew there and asked him if he liked the club.
5. I remembered to face somebody I was talking to and not turn in the other direction.
6. I tried to speak up more loudly when I answered a question in class.
7. I practiced making eye contact with the teacher when she was talking to me.
8. [Easiest] I said hi to a kid in my class who I usually don't talk to, even though he didn't say hi first.

The Child Who Has a Panic Attack

You read in an earlier chapter about Becca, a 13-year-old, whose anxiety overtook her when she was in confined places, especially subways. Her fearfulness manifested itself in overwhelming thoughts of impending disaster and in physical distress. At such moments, the child feels a desperate need to escape, though escaping only functions to make things worse.

Here is a Bravery Ladder we developed for another adolescent, a boy old enough to ride the subway alone, though he was terrified to do so. As was true for Becca, he panicked in situations in which he felt "totally trapped," he said, unable to leave. Those situations sometimes occurred at school; he would simply walk out of his classroom and out of the building, which was clearly not in his best interests.

The steps on his ladder required him to stay put for increasingly longer stretches of time when he felt "trapped."

The Bravery Ladder

1. [Hardest] I went to school and stayed in my classes for six hours.
2. I went on a whale watch boat ride that lasted four hours.
3. I went on a trolley tour of the city that lasted an hour and a half.
4. I went on a long car trip and sat in the backseat.
5. I rode the subway alone for at least thirty minutes and stayed in the situation until my anxiety came down.
6. I rode the subway for at least thirty minutes with my mom until my anxiety came down.
7. I went more than one stop on the subway with my mom.
8. [Easiest] I went one stop on the subway with my parents.

The Child Who's Afraid of Public Speaking

Difficulty speaking or performing in public or reading aloud before a group is a common expression of social phobia. The child is perfectly fine in most social interactions, but loses all confidence when called on to present herself before an audience. Catastrophizing thoughts take over: everyone is looking at her, she'll make a mistake, she'll faint. Lila, a teenager, was frustrated and angry at herself for these reactions, which she nevertheless found impossible to control.

This was a girl with many talents and enthusiasms. She wrote poetry; played the piano expertly, having taken lessons since age 3; was an outstanding student. Lila had passed up several opportunities that appealed to her, including joining the debate society in school, because of her anxiety. She was convinced that she would fall apart at crucial moments. Like some young people who are frustrated by their fears and highly determined to overcome them, she had tried to address the problem once or twice by challenging herself in the most difficult circumstances—essentially starting off at the top of a Bravery Ladder. That didn't work well.

We laid out an exposure plan that promised a greater possibility of success, beginning small in intimate settings.

The Bravery Ladder

1. [Hardest] I will help the principal make the announcements to the whole school the next time there's a schoolwide assembly.

2. I will give a fifteen-minute talk to my social studies class by myself.

3. I will give a fifteen-minute talk to my social studies class with a partner.

4. I will volunteer to complete a math problem at the chalk-board in front of the class.

5. I will read aloud to the class the next time my English teacher wants us to read a poetry passage.

6. I will invite my grandparents over and recite a poetry passage, and this time I will purposely try to make a mistake or mispronounce a word.

7. I will invite the neighbors over and play one piano piece for them. Before playing I'll say a few sentences about the piece I chose to play and why I like it.

8. I will give a five-minute speech to my family while they eat dinner.

9. I will tape-record myself giving a speech and play the tape for my family during dinner.

10. [Easiest] I will prepare a five-minute speech that I rehearse in front of my bedroom mirror.

The Child Who Has a Fear of Vomiting

For reasons that are not entirely clear, fear of vomiting is extremely common among young children these days. Perhaps an increased awareness of how to prevent getting sick has contributed to it. Throwing up is also an unpleasant, somewhat explosive bodily function that probably feels uncontrollable to kids, and thus especially scary. Often the child who becomes anxious has seen or heard someone else vomit, and believes that she, too, will be sick, and if she does get sick it'll be the worst thing in the world.

Creating a Bravery Ladder is a challenge because the natural top of the fear-and-avoidance hierarchy would be the child vomiting herself without panicking, and some exposure therapy with adults who experience this fear actually involves giving the individual syrup of ipecac, an emetic to induce vomiting. In the clinic, we don't do that, but we have developed a series of steps that help a youngster realize that, yes, vomiting is uncomfortable; yes, it's kind of gross, and nobody really likes it; but it happens and people get over it and move on.

A version of the Bravery Ladder below was developed for a girl who came to the clinic after her anxiety had seriously impaired her functioning and was making family life miserable. Emma, age 8, had seen a classmate vomit, and now she wanted to avoid school; at the time I met her, she hadn't been to class in two weeks. Each morning, she asked her parents worry questions: "Am I going to be sick? Feel my head. Am I warm? Do I have a fever?" They, obligingly, felt her head, told her she wasn't warm, she wasn't going to be sick. Emma replied, "Okay, thanks for telling me."

Her questions got more involved, however, and her need for reassurance expanded. "Can you just take a walk with me around the block?" Emma pleaded. Soon the walk around the block became a walk around the neighborhood for half an hour or more, to calm her down. Her parents, again, obliged.

They were encouraged to stop answering their daughter's worry questions, because their answers were only reinforcing her anxiety; whatever they told her, Emma was soon again fearful about getting sick. Mom and dad were able to stop the reassurances, until Emma started bringing on more anxiety. "Oh, I'm really going to be sick," she'd say. "You've got to help me. I'm having hallucinations." She wasn't hallucinating, but she was screaming, verging on a tantrum. Emma had learned that if she made enough of a fuss, eventually her parents would jump in and make it better by acceding to her demands. Emma was essentially running the household.

Such escalation is a behavioral phenomenon called a "response burst," and it is not uncommon when treating childhood anxiety disorders: take away the reinforcement of negative behaviors, and the behaviors get more frequent and more extreme. In time, however, when they are no longer fed with attention, they disappear.

Emma's parents needed to take back the reins. They'd still give her attention, but attention for trying to use the skills I was teaching her. They were also encouraged to provide more structure for their child, making sure she had a good breakfast every morning, for example, during which they would not engage in any conversations about vomiting and sickness and would bring up three other things to talk about.

Emma had to learn emotion-focused coping skills. She and I worked together on coming up with more accurate statements she could be thinking to herself. We played detective, looking at her thoughts and figuring out if they were true or just beliefs. In fact, she said, even though she thought she would be sick every morning, she never did get sick. She practiced relaxation skills at night before bed.

I told Emma her parents would not be responding to all her worry questions and demands, but they would be giving her tons of hugs when she took a step on her Bravery Ladder. We have certificates for kids who complete a course in dealing with their fears, and she loved hearing that. She wanted to earn a certificate! I promised her we could also have a bravery party at the end when she got better.

We brainstormed steps, and Emma said that maybe she could draw a picture of a kid who might be getting sick, so we started there. Even looking at pictures was hard, but she persevered. Halfway up the ladder, Emma looked at the "pretend vomit" we concoct at our clinic (probably a step you'd rather not do at home—but you can!), a realistic-looking mixture of bits of cooked vegetables, creamed soup, and whatnot. She managed it well.

In a short time, Emma was in good spirits and clearly feeling better. Her parents were thrilled. Life was assuming normalcy again.

The Bravery Ladder

1. [Hardest] I felt a little sick, but I stayed in the cafeteria for the whole lunch period.
2. I talked to a classmate at school who had vomited.
3. I watched a movie that showed someone vomiting.
4. I looked at a photograph of someone throwing up.
5. I drew a picture of someone vomiting into a toilet.
6. I drew a picture of someone who was going to be sick.
7. I imagined someone throwing up.
8. [Easiest] I didn't ask my mom this morning if I was going to be sick.

Celebrating Success

Climbing a Bravery Ladder takes determination, effort, and courage. If your child has been successful at this hard task, celebrate her achievement. In our clinic, we'll throw a party.

Mya, an 11-year-old, had great difficulty separating from her mom, which was a problem when it came to parties and other peer activities. Her family was deeply religious, very active in their church, and this connection also set her somewhat apart. If she brought up anything related to her religion, the children she came in contact with tended to regard her suspiciously. Mya's interests were not typical of her age group. I noticed that she liked little-girl things, playing with dolls and collecting stuffed animals. That was not inappropriate, but her classmates were moving into preteen areas, so she stood out. One day she took one of her animals to school, and kids made fun of her. Mya felt rejected.

Her loving parents were heartbroken, especially since their older daughter was able to make friends comfortably. They were at a loss as to how to encourage Mya. They didn't want to push her, because she'd become upset and teary, so they let her be. She hung around with her mother all summer, following her on errands. She was a lonely little girl.

I tried to teach Mya some social skills, how to get along with other children, while still letting them know who she was. We talked about seeking out kids who gave her a clue that they might enjoy the kinds of things she did, and about the best ways to approach possible new friends. We didn't want to change this very sweet young girl, just help her learn how to participate in activities and conversations that were current for her age group.

Her parents embraced the whole process. They gradually encouraged her to try difficult situations, but took a step back themselves and let Mya realize she could regulate her emotions on her own. When Mya went to a birthday party, we had mom wait in the car outside for a few minutes, then come back later. The child was afraid no one at the party or no other mom would understand that this was hard for her and no one would help her if she got sad, but she managed.

She made great strides. One day toward the end of treatment Mya arrived for a session with a picture of two little feet she had painted using her knuckles. These, she said, were her baby steps, and she learned that taking baby steps to success was what was working for her. She made me a baby-steps-to-success card.

At the very end of Mya's treatment, we planned a "bravery party" at the clinic, pizza with her mom and dad. Mya called later and asked, "Would it be all right if I bring some other people? My sister and maybe one other person?" No problem, I said. On party day, mom and dad arrived, as well as Mya's sister and grandparents, their pastor, and several people from church. I quickly had to grab a larger room. Mya's mom brought one of those cakes with a photo decoration on top, and there was a picture of Mya and me in colorful icing.

All the people there, who loved this girl and had watched her struggle for so long, rose one at a time and gave a brief talk about what positive changes they noticed in Mya. She was having so much more fun now, they said. She was so friendly. Her big sister said, "I love my sister and it made me sad to see her unhappy, and now I see she spends time with other kids and I think she's so brave."

Not a dry eye in the house.

I had asked Dr. David Barlow, the director of our center, to stop by. I wanted Mya to see that this was such a big deal that the director himself wanted to come to her party. He walked in saying, "I understand there's been a very successful kid here," and he shook her hand. Mya beamed.

I still have the baby-steps-to-success card that she made me. A nice message to all children and to their parents: take small steps to a big goal. That's how growing up brave works.

CHAPTER 11

Halfway to Adulthood

Combating the Fears of Adolescence

Teenagers who come for treatment at our center can present with a range of anxiety disorders similar to those of younger children; however, social phobia and panic disorder are the two that become more prevalent in adolescence. These years hold their own particular stresses, when kids are further individuating themselves from parents and striving for greater independence, when making friends and perhaps having a girlfriend or boyfriend becomes more important. Panic attacks and social phobia, or other anxiety disorders, can squelch those developmentally appropriate tasks of adolescence.

The process of getting better embraces all the concepts and strategies I have been describing: understanding the cycle of anxiety, and how the components of thoughts, feelings, and behaviors work together to perpetuate — or reduce — fearfulness; using cognitive restructuring, or "detective skills," to change maladaptive thinking; habituating to physical sensations through interoceptive exercises and practicing relaxation and breathing techniques; engaging in controlled exposures to the situations that terrify.

But a 15- or 16-year-old's life obviously differs from a 5- or 6-year-old's in significant ways, and a parent's response to the adolescent's problems and efforts to solve them can be tricky to negotiate. In our work with families, we have just begun to explore how much parental involvement is desirable. Some previous studies comparing treatment with and without parental involvement have shown clearly that kids do better when parents are part of the picture. Especially with younger children, parent participation seems to be directly relevant, so mom or dad can follow through and continue to foster the skills. With adolescents, the optimal parent component is a little harder to gauge.

To be truly helpful to your struggling teen, there are a few basics to strive for: respect your child's developmental stage; notice if you are playing the role of the ever-ready "safety object," unwittingly preventing him from productively facing his fears; learn the "language" of coping skills; and, first, inform yourself. What goes on in the mind and behavior of an anxious adolescent? What are the symptoms of panic and social phobia, the two anxiety disorders that commonly begin in adolescence?

Panic Attacks and Panic Disorder

Before a teenager begins treatment, he completes questionnaires that help us determine the severity of his problem. As any parent will attest to, most of us have experienced intense, over-the-top fear in reaction to a particular circumstance. And we can probably recall the uncomfortable or upsetting feelings that swept through our bodies. I've mentioned many of these symptoms in previous chapters: a rapid heartbeat, shaking, shortness of breath, sweating, dizziness, tingling sensations or numbness, chest pain, chills or hot flushes, perhaps fear of losing control or even dying. The symptoms typically peak within about ten minutes from the onset. That's a panic attack.

If the teenager I'm seeing—Jeremy, we'll call him—describes an episode he's been through (or more than one), and remembers when it began and that he felt at least four of the symptoms on our checklist, we agree that he has, indeed, had a panic attack (or attacks). It may have started innocently or normally enough. That is, the trigger was recognizable. Perhaps Jeremy was nervous about giving an oral presentation in class, and he'd been up half the night before worrying about it. While speaking, he became flustered and lost his place; his heart was pounding, he was light-headed, and so on. He made it through his presentation, but believed he had embarrassed himself horribly in front of the class and the teacher.

To discover if a child's attacks can accurately be called part of "panic disorder" (PD), we explore further. For a diagnosis of PD, the teenager will have had at least two attacks that seemed to come out of nowhere. Jeremy may at some later point have been sitting in class or walking around the mall, and the symptoms suddenly, with no connection to an immediate event, overwhelmed him. And then, the attack so rattled him that for a period of at least one month afterward he lived in dread of another one. An extremely common response to that fear is agoraphobia, or avoiding places or situations the teen thinks might again cause a rush of these frightening feelings.

For many adolescents with PD, agoraphobia significantly interferes not only with feelings of well-being, but with participation in their young lives. I have worked with kids who had to flee the scene—or never approached it in the first place—while waiting in line for take-out food, eating in a restaurant, attending a dance, or staying at home alone. Terrified at bringing on the hot flushes or rapid heartbeat, they will not take a hot shower, drink coffee, or watch a scary movie. Some end up not going to the mall, the movies, or school.

Lauren was only 13 when she had her first panic attack. In a difficult math class one day, her heart started racing and she couldn't catch her breath, and she asked for a pass to the nurse's office. She thought these feelings might have been caused by the breakfast she had, and from then on she refrained from eating anything on a weekday morning. But she began to notice the same symptoms starting for no apparent reason at different times—in other classes at school, on the bus, and while shopping in a convenience store. What alarmed her most was the day she was at home on a pleasant Saturday morning, enjoying the pancakes her father had made her, sitting comfortably in her pajamas—the most relaxed place she could possibly be—and she experienced a full panic attack.

Lauren was convinced something was wrong with her heart. Her parents took her to the doctor and then to a heart specialist, and all medical reports came back normal. Her mother read that Lauren's symptoms could be related to anxiety or panic, and she brought her daughter to our center for an evaluation.

At her first session in our intensive-treatment program for adolescents with PD and agoraphobia, Lauren reported that her panic had caused her to avoid many things, including getting a haircut, remaining in her classes, and going to parties. If she did participate in one of those activities, it had to be with "modifications," as she called them—sitting on the aisle, holding her cell phone, and carrying a special juice. She had also begun to require that at least one friend who "understood" her be present if she needed to go anywhere. Lauren was immediately on the phone with her mother any time she felt the symptoms starting.

This young girl did well in treatment, though it wasn't easy for her. She went on exposures, putting herself intentionally in the situations she stayed away from out of fear, and habituating herself to the panicky sensations. At one point, I took her for a haircut (she hadn't had one in a long time and desperately wanted one). Halfway through, Lauren ran out of the salon with one side of her hair cut and the other not, hair still wet, the drape falling from her shoulders. This was quite a scene in busy Kenmore Square, game day for the Red Sox, with crowds milling about. I tried to help her regain her strength, resume her exposure, go back inside, and ride the wave of anxiety without denying her feelings. She did return to the salon and got the rest of her hair cut. She felt so proud of herself. In time, Lauren gained mastery over her attacks.

As part of the treatment, her mother learned about the anatomy, so to speak, of panic, and that the physical feelings brought on by the body's fight-or-flight response to a perceived threat were not harmful to her daughter.

Social Phobia

Excessive timidity and fearfulness about engaging with others can take a toll on children from very young ages. If the child with perhaps a naturally inhibited temperament does not, over the years of childhood, pick up and practice social skills—the kind of "how to talk to people" tactics I described in a Bravery Ladder in chapter 10—he can end up outcast as a teen. Some kids have mastered basic skills, but their maladaptive "worry thoughts" about whether others will accept them or whether they will embarrass themselves can interfere in their ability to participate in normal teenage interactions. They begin to avoid the very activities they should be enjoying in the teen years. Socially phobic adolescents might live very much in their own heads, with exaggerated anticipation of rejection. That's happening just at the stage when establishing positive peer connections is critical to psychological development, moving from childhood to young adult.

Daniel, 16, suffering from social anxiety, often refused to go to school. His reluctance grew into a full-blown problem when the principal threatened suspension or legal action if the boy did not begin attending more regularly. Daniel started having a panic attack each time he even thought of school, and his parents were nervously considering the possibility of home-schooling their son.

He was coping with his miseries by spending a lot of time in online chatrooms, where he didn't have to deal with live communications. There he connected with another boy about the same age who lived in his area, and he referred to this boy as his best friend, though they never talked in person. Eventually they did meet, and Daniel began visiting at the boy's house, often letting his parents know he'd be staying overnight, which pleased his mom and dad. He was finally making friends, they thought. What they didn't know was that the teens were drinking alcohol at least three times a week and smoking pot when they could get it.

Daniel had never been in therapy to deal with the underlying issues that had led to his fears and subsequent isolation, but eventually he admitted to his parents—this was a brave step—that he could use some help. They were thrilled to start the process at our anxiety treatment center. During his initial assessment, he talked about his feelings and substance abuse in terms identical to those used by Leah, the girl I described in chapter 1: drinking and smoking helped him "numb away" the anxiety he felt about school and being around other kids.

On day one of a group treatment for social anxiety disorder, Daniel sat with his head down, refusing to look at anyone. The only thing that helped him talk, he said, was figuring that some other kids there were more awkward and "worse off" than he was. Gradually, he learned to combat the anxious thoughts that floated through his mind continually: "I will never be accepted" and "I am strange and weird." One of his goals, he announced, was to get back to work—he'd briefly held a part-time job as a stock boy—and the group members encouraged him to apply in different stores.

We practiced social skills—making eye contact, daring to smile. We also encouraged Daniel and the others in the group to challenge some of the negative thoughts they had believed were "true," and the teens worked together to help each other recalibrate new, more accurate thoughts. Eventually, Daniel landed another stock job, and he showed one of his first sparks of excitement at our next session when he reported that he actually had had a short conversation with another worker in the store. As his overall anxiety began to decrease, he reported that he wasn't smoking pot anymore and he no longer felt "depressed." Toward the end of treatment, he told the group that a few of the cashiers and other stock workers at the supermarket had asked him to go out to a restaurant with them after work one night.

A big concern for Daniel's parents had been their son's graduation from high school. He did finish out his remaining year and a half, which pleased his mom and dad enormously.

How and Why Parents and Teen May Disagree

When kids are young, parents tend to be pretty accurate report-ers of what's troubling them. Mom and dad, after all, are largely running their child's daily life and are in touch with his develop-mental stage. And since 5-year-old Jimmy may not be able to describe his thoughts and feelings, at the beginning of treatment we rely mainly on his parents' report. When Jimmy reaches age 8 or 9, I'll usually question both him and his parents — what's been happening? how did the problem start? — and often I find over-laps between the two accounts.

In adolescence, parents and their teens sometimes see things differently. Mom might be saying, "My son worries, he's anxious all the time, he's a wreck, this is serious." Son, meanwhile, says, "Yeah, in fact I worry a lot, but it's not a big deal, it's not actually interfering with my life at all." Or the parent says, "He's kind of a loner, but it doesn't bother him, he's doing just fine," while the boy says, "It does bother me. My mother doesn't understand any-thing. She doesn't get it."

The discrepancy may exist for various reasons. Some adoles-cents disclose less than others. During the stage of separation and individuation, they may not want to clue their parents in to their problems. At the same time, parents may be at least partly in the dark about the child's comings and goings, school routines, the kids he likes or doesn't like, where he eats lunch, and other details of the day. It also may be the case that an adolescent's seeming anxiety or anxious behavior is upsetting the parent more than the child, and mom is dealing with her distress by either working herself into a mental frenzy or denying that anything is wrong.

The two children I've described, Lauren and Daniel, were

fairly candid with their parents. Many children will not be. Suppose your teenager isn't telling you much; you do sense that life is not going well for him and you've thought so for some time, and you're reasonably certain that you are neither overreacting nor underreacting. Put yourself in the picture.

"How Can I Help?"

If you've had a decent relationship with your child through the years and established an atmosphere of positive communication and warmth, you can do this. Even if he's going through a "teen thing," needing to separate, maybe giving every indication that he can't stand his parents, he'll listen. And I think you can be absolutely frank in starting the conversation and getting to the core of your concern: "I'm noticing that you seem pretty sad. Parents do pay attention to these kinds of things about their kids, and I want to make sure that we talk about it. Maybe I can help you with this or we can find someone who can."

Or the conversation opener might be: "I know you like playing on the computer, you can do it for hours, but it's really important for kids your age to get out a little more. You know that Dad and I are pretty smart about what's good for you, and we believe this will be good for you, too, spending time with friends. Let's brainstorm, think of somebody you'd like to get together with."

The talk might continue something like this:

Teen: No, I'm okay. I don't need that. I have friends online.
Parent: It's fine to be on the computer, but I want you to limit that to, say, two hours a day. Once a week, let's try this. You make an arrangement to see friends face-to-face, outside of school.

Teen: I don't want to.

Parent (forging on): Are there some kids you feel especially comfortable around?

Teen: I'm comfortable around everybody.

Parent: What about Jared? He seems like a nice kid. How about going to a movie with Jared?

Teen: Nah, I don't think he wants to.

Parent: Let's try it. Let's give it a shot.

Teen: He won't want to go.

The story behind this exchange is that your child may be able to think of one or two peers he wouldn't mind spending time with, but he won't reach out for fear of rejection. Ask some "what's the worst you can expect?" anti-catastrophizing questions.

Parent: Well, what might happen if you call him?

Teen: I dunno. He'll say he's busy.

Parent: That doesn't sound so terrible. What could you say if that did happen?

If all this goes nowhere, and you know Jared, perhaps, with your son's permission, you can call that boy's parent, and ask, "I'm trying to get my son out a little more. Any chance we could hook the boys up for a movie? I'm willing to drive both ways. I know he likes your son." You need not disclose any more than that; you're not saying, "My child has social phobia, and I want your child to be his exposure!" This is a casual suggestion and offer.

If your child continues to resist the whole idea, try to engage him in a conversation about what, exactly, he finds most nerve-wracking about going to the movies with another child.

Socially challenged kids have different and specific fears. For many adolescents, the prospect of setting up an arrangement or the anticipation of the event is what's most scary. Once under way, it's not so bad. Other kids worry that they won't know what to say when they meet up with a friend or are sitting and waiting for the movie to start. In treatment, we talk about these issues a lot with teens who experience social phobia, reviewing the possible details and nuances of a situation.

If your teen is willing to open up to you and talk a little about his particular anxieties, together you may be able to figure out some smaller steps that will make him feel more confident. Role-play with him, focusing on what part is the most difficult. Rehearse the dialogue.

Parent: Okay, this is the script of what will happen when you get there. You'll say hi to your friend. You'll say, "Want to get some food?" You'll go up to the concession stand and buy popcorn. You pay for it. You get your change. Walk in.

Or: You sound worried about what you'll talk about. Maybe we can brainstorm a few good topics together.

Discuss some of the possibilities, probabilities, and solutions ahead of time. Create the expectation of success. And then continue to make plans for exposures within a reasonable schedule, thinking ahead.

Young teens for the most part depend on their parents to transport them, and with a phobic child who's not enjoying much social interaction, it's especially critical for mom or dad to be available. It takes effort. You can feel you're going uphill to engineer these kinds of opportunities. I've seen too often parents who haven't followed through; life is busy, the adolescent is resistant, it's so much easier to just let him stay home, parked in front of the computer.

When your child has the chance to go to a movie with other kids, or to a party or a teen dance or a music concert—a chance to make a friend, to become more socially integrated—make the time to help him get there.

The Language of Panic

If you will be helping your teen with feelings of panic, review the information in chapters 1 and 8, and at a calm time, talk over with her these critical facts about adjusting to physical feelings— recognizing the adaptive nature of the fight-or-flight system, staying in the moment, riding it out, and gauging anxiety on the 0-to-8 scale. She can appreciate that panic results from a combination of physical sensations and fear in response to them, which increases the intensity of the sensations, which in turn increases fearfulness. And she might benefit from the interoceptive exposure exercise described earlier, intentionally bringing on the feelings in a controlled situation and learning "not to let what we feel scare us." When an adolescent has completed therapy at our center, we encourage her parent to take over the role of therapist, in a sense, helping the child set up appropriate exposures and coaching her through them.

Witnessing or hearing from a child in the midst of a panic attack can be hugely disturbing to parents. They may worry that she's in real danger and might actually be about to faint or even die, as she fears. The mothers and fathers I've met want desperately to help their teen but often have no idea how and become caught up in the hysteria of the moment. In one family, the mother literally rocked her panicking 15-year-old daughter on her lap, as if she were a baby, murmuring, "Shhh, shhh." This parent said, "I didn't know what else to do to help. This was what I used to do when she was little and got upset. This was how I quieted her."

One of the best strategies is knowing what to say—and what not to say—if you get a panicked phone call, and putting the anxiety-intensity scale to good use.

Calling a parent or friend, the "safety person," is probably the number one instinct among adolescents when they experience fear of an attack. With cell phones it's ever easier to be instantly in touch with mom or dad, relying on the parent to talk them through it and be a calming force. If you're on the receiving end of one of those calls, it can be terrifying to hear your child gasping or crying and saying, "I think I'm dying!" The conversation might continue this way:

Mom: You can't breathe? What's the matter? Where are you?

Teen: I'm in the mall. I don't feel right. My chest hurts and my heart is pounding.

Mom: I'll be right there. Should I call the doctor?

Teen: Do I need a doctor? Maybe I'm having a heart attack.

Mom: Are you hyperventilating? Is this just one of your anxiety attacks?

Teen: No, I think I'm really sick this time. Something feels wrong. You have to come get me.

Mom: Okay, just try breathing slowly, in and out, until I get there. I'll call the doctor.

Teen: I am trying, but I can't catch my breath!

We call this the downward spiral of panic: Mom first reacts to the child's initial outburst with her own panicky remarks, which escalate the child's panic, and the cycle continues.

Take preventive steps—again, when life is calm—to lessen the possibility of this kind of exchange. Talk to your teen about the concepts of probability overestimation and catastrophizing, and about the usefulness of cognitive restructuring to decrease her anxieties. She's nervous about going to a school dance, let's say. Ask what's worrying her, and she may reply that she knows she'll feel sick and she might faint or she'll probably throw up. Lead her through a "using my detective skills" dialogue:

Mom: I suppose that's a possibility. But is it also possible that you'll go to the dance and not feel sick and actually have a good time?

Teen: I guess so.

Mom: You did go to one of these dances before, remember? Did you feel sick then?

Teen: No, I was kind of nervous, but I didn't get sick.

Mom: So maybe you're overestimating the probability that you'll get sick and throw up?

Teen: Okay, but it could still happen.

Mom now encourages her teen to review her catastrophic thinking.

Mom: Well, suppose you did panic and you fainted or you threw up. What's the worst thing about that?

Teen: I'll look like an idiot. My friends will want nothing to do with me. People will think I'm diseased and strange.

Mom: Suppose some kids did think you were strange. Does it matter so much?

Teen: I guess not, but I'd be so embarrassed.

Mom: Have you ever been embarrassed before?

Teen: Yeah, sure.

Mom: And you lived to tell the tale, right? Could you cope with feeling embarrassed for a while?

Teen: I suppose so.

The child learns to recognize that the worst thing she imagines probably won't happen, but if it did she could handle it. During such a conversation, it's helpful to bring up the point that even if she does not use catastrophic thinking, she may still feel some anxiety when going to the dance, and that's okay. For kids with panic, learning to cope effectively in difficult situations can happen gradually. Most important, the adolescent should stay in the situation until her anxiety decreases from the peak "freaking out" level to a midpoint, from an 8 to about a 3 or 4.

When you and your adolescent develop a "common language" of anxiety, and what works to reduce it, the panicky phone conversation I described might proceed something like this:

Teen: I can't breathe!

Mom: You're starting to feel really anxious. That makes sense. You haven't been to the mall in a long time. Remember what we've talked about. Use your skills to change any worry thoughts you're having that may not be true.

Teen: I can't do it. I tried. I can't calm down!

Mom: Okay, I hear you. It sounds like you're at an 8 now.

Teen: Yeah, it's really bad. I need to get out of here!

Mom: I know you're uncomfortable, but you know that how you're feeling isn't going to hurt you. Notice how long it takes for your anxiety to come down to a 6. Remember, if you leave now, it's still going to feel harder the next time you go to the mall. You can do this. You've done it before.

Teen (a few minutes later): Yes, I actually think it's coming down now.

Mom: Good for you. I'm very proud of you.

Remind your child of what she already knows (because you've talked this over in the past): scary physical feelings are caused by anxiety, not heart failure or another dire illness; they are unpleasant, but she's not in any danger; they will soon go away all by themselves; sticking it out makes her stronger. You are also telling her that you know she's capable of handling the situation.

You can help your child set up exposures. But we know that teens want some independence and control over the experience. If mom is hovering, saying, "It's time to practice your exposure," the child might reject the whole idea, or invent excuses: she's too busy right now, she's under a lot of stress, she doesn't feel well.

Give her room to choose the tasks she will confront, but let her know that taking the bull by the horns, facing her fears instead of avoiding them—and taking advantage of your support and assistance—will help her move forward. She might mainly want your support in the form of drives to a friend's house or to the mall, which is fine.

Relaxation and Breathing Techniques for Teens

In one of our studies of teens with panic, we asked which skill they thought worked best for them, which strategies or approaches were most successful in helping them feel better. Many teens responded that learning to relax and bring on calm feelings was the most useful tool they'd picked up. This was somewhat surprising. We might have predicted cognitive restructuring—the mental work—but these adolescents really liked the more physical technique.

In chapter 8, you read the "I Can Relax!" exercise designed to lead children through progressive muscle relaxation. The images are most appealing to youngsters; adolescents might find them too "little kid." But suggest to your teen that he read over the exercise, or read it together, and see if he'd like to redesign the steps in a script that suits him. Perhaps he'd imagine himself at his favorite beach, listening to the crashing of the waves. Or he's on a soft couch under a pile of cozy blankets. Get creative and have a little fun with this technique, and record the script if he wants. The pictures may change, but the process remains the same: work each muscle group one at a time, tensing the muscles for a few seconds and then gradually releasing the tension.

Many kids with panic disorder are especially sensitive to breathing-related cues or have a tendency to hyperventilate — overbreathe — during an attack or in fear of an impending attack. Some with anxiety tend to overbreathe even when not in the grip of panic fears. Adolescents for the most part are aware enough to benefit from a simple explanation of the physiology of hyperventilation, what exactly is going on in the body when breathing differs from its normal pattern. If "I can't catch my breath!" is one of your child's most terrifying symptoms, help her understand the following facts:

• Breathing is how the body takes in oxygen and gets rid of carbon dioxide. Breath in = oxygen; breath out = carbon dioxide.

• When your breathing is a little off — maybe deep and rapid, like panting; or rapid and shallow; or even when you're sighing or yawning a lot — you're getting rid of more than the usual amount of carbon dioxide.

• A lowered level of carbon dioxide in the body can produce sensations such as dizziness, heart palpitations, and tingling.

• You may not even be aware that you are hyperventilating, but these sudden unexpected symptoms can trigger a panic attack, one that seems to come out of the blue, not related to any situation you're in.

• Hyperventilating is not dangerous. Once you stop over-breathing, your body returns to its normal state and your symptoms fade away.

Kids who overbreathe tend to use their chest muscles rather than their diaphragms, and that can add to anxiety by causing tightness or even pain in the chest. Since breathing is one of the few automatic bodily processes over which we humans are able to exert voluntary control, we can work on better breathing. Coach your teen through the exercise in the box below. When she's learned the skill, she should continue to practice it regularly.

A Slow-Breathing Exercise

When taking air into our lungs, the abdominal muscles should move, not the chest muscles. Explain to your child that this diaphragmatic breathing can help decrease the frequency of sensations that may be triggering panic. Here's how the exercise goes:

• In a comfortable position, relax for a few seconds.
• Breathe, smoothly and evenly, at your normal rate and depth (about ten to fourteen breaths per minute).
• Place one hand on your chest and the other hand on your diaphragm, just above the navel.
• As you inhale, feel the hand on your diaphragm moving up while the hand on your chest remains still.
• Continue the exercise for about one minute.

Your child may experience some minor dizziness or breathlessness during the routine. That's normal. If the symptoms are highly upsetting to her, she can stop for a few seconds until they decrease, and then begin again.

Living with an Anxious Teen

Adolescents can try our patience and make us question our parenting skills in the best of circumstances. Life with an adolescent with an anxiety disorder can be doubly difficult. A few rules to keep in mind:

• *Be empathetic.* Facing up to fears is terribly difficult. If your teen has gone on an exposure and he's tired and acting stressed out, appreciate his feelings. You don't have to tiptoe around on eggshells or be overly solicitous, but let him know that you understand he's had a tough time. Tell him, "You did some really hard stuff today. It's no wonder you're tired."

• *Expect a little pushback.* Sometimes kids can get angry about having to do the hard things. They might be irritable and taking it out on mom or dad. We say that the "fight" side of the fight-or-flight response comes out, which is actually a good sign. Your child is pushing himself to confront his anxieties.

• *Maintain realistic expectations, and make sure your teen does, too.* Teens with anxiety may be constantly improving in small, gradual steps, even if it doesn't always look that way. Symptom fluctuations are not uncommon. Periods of stress—school demands, problems with friends, problems at home—put him at increased susceptibility to feeling anxious. Don't let him become discouraged or blame himself for "failing" or being "weak."

• *Praise what's going right.* Your adolescent might tend to be hard on himself and focus on everything he can't do or everything he's getting wrong. Of course, you will give your child a little "bravo" when he's faced up to his fear with determination. But also give him some words of praise if he's remembered to take out the trash or clean up his room. A few specific compliments—the labeled praise I described earlier—are great positive reinforcers.

• *Set limits*. Many parents I meet in the course of treating an adolescent are inclined to make allowances for their child in various contexts, perhaps tolerating some obnoxious or oppositional behavior that normally they wouldn't. "She's trying to be more socially outgoing," they think. "She's upset. I don't want to bug her or nag her about other stuff." But your teen doesn't get a free pass because she's fighting an anxiety disorder. Like all parents, you probably have some household rules that family members are expected to follow: people have to go to bed at appropriate times; kids have to go to school.

• *Expect success*. Another way of putting it: do not anticipate your adolescent's anxiety and take measures to head it off. One mother, for example, sent regrets on her child's behalf to an invitation to a sixteenth birthday party a colleague was organizing for her daughter. Let your child know that while she might feel anxious and uncomfortable, she can deal. And she might even end up having fun.

The Changing Relationship

Most teenagers typically prefer not to spend a whole lot of downtime with their parents. Taking in a popular movie with mom or dad might seem unappealing. Some adolescents with heightened anxiety, however, want to stick close to home base and the parental safety object. The teen might say to a peer, "No, I don't want to go, I just feel like hanging out at home today." Or to mom, "I'll go to the mall with some kids, but I want you to come, too." For the parent, it can feel reinforcing, offering a sense of purpose

(I'm still important in her life). When the child's anxiety lessens, the parent is oddly unsettled.

I realized the significance of this issue only after talking with a number of parents who described their strong and often conflicted emotions. One mother said, "It's not that I'm not grateful and thankful my child is better, but I'm a little sad." Another, in tears, said, "I think I'm crying because I'm so happy my daughter has gotten her life back, but I'm also missing the time I used to spend with her. I'm not sure what I can do with her. It's almost like I don't know how to talk to her anymore." Another: "I always told him, You need me, you call me. Now he doesn't call throughout the day. Which I know is a good thing, but still."

Social phobia and panic disorder tend to throw off course the normal and necessary and sometimes messy process of separation during adolescence. When a kid has done well in treatment and is making great strides in overcoming her fears, beginning to have a more independent life, we might have to have a discussion about the changing parent-child dynamic. I encourage both parties, parent and child, to talk candidly, face-to-face, about their feelings. The teen might say, "It's not that I don't love you. I still want to do stuff with you." Mom might say, "I'm really glad that you're doing so well that you can go out with friends, but I sort of miss having you home on Saturday night."

Then we consider how to change the picture. Anxiety was, in a sense, some of the "glue" that kept the relationship close, with teen feeling safe and parent feeling needed. If the interfering anxiety goes away, what can replace it?

Think about what the two of you can enjoy together. I've had kids say, "I'm really pretty okay now. I can keep my job and I can go out with my friends. I want to do all that, but maybe Mom and I can do something on Sunday afternoons. That's when most of the kids I know are with their families. Maybe we can go shopping."

One girl and her mother decided to take a cooking class. Another parent and child made regular "dates" to spend an hour or two at the art museum on weekends.

It's wise to be aware that sibling dynamics might undergo changes, too, and that the non-anxious child will be adapting to a different order of things. In treatment, the adolescent is never seen in isolation, but considered as part of the family system, and I may hear about the brother or sister who has a lingering resentment of the attention given to the child with the problems, aware of the general heightened tension around the home. Or I learn that brother or sister was regularly utilized by the anxious child for assistance or avoidance; the sibling played the role of safety object. The improved landscape might be good for everyone, but siblings who are also shifting gears can need some support and understanding, too.

Reaching Out

For Hank, 17, riding elevators brought on panic attacks. He skipped his high school prom at the Marriott Copley Place in downtown Boston. During a reconnaissance mission early on, he realized that the dance would be held on a floor reachable only by elevator, and so he opted out of the evening. His girlfriend wanted to take him to a "high above the city" restaurant for his birthday, but, not wanting her to know about his phobia, he made a lame excuse to avoid the dinner.

Hank was an extremely smart kid, top of his class, and wanted to attend MIT and head toward a future in math or science. When it came to college applications, however, he considered campuses depending on how many tall buildings each had, and he settled on a couple of schools in the Midwest, very low to the ground, no elevators. All this began to seem ridiculous to Hank. Not comfortable discussing his panic with his parents, he researched on his own, found us online, called the center, and said, "I can't ride in elevators. I need help."

His problem had been going on since childhood, he said, and the way it took root demonstrates how fears can be acquired just by listening or reacting to the fears of people around one. When she was a child, Hank's mother caught her arm in an elevator, a terrifying experience then but one that she had turned into a good story in retrospect. An animated and gregarious woman, she loved to repeat the tale at Thanksgiving dinner and other family gatherings: "Have I ever told you about the time...?" She usually had her audience laughing. Her young son was horrified.

Hank's mother was required to come to the center, too, because of his age, and she readily agreed, saying, "I'm very proud of my son. I had no idea this was affecting him so much. I should probably be getting treatment myself!"

Hank and I went all around the Boston area visiting buildings and taking small elevator hops—to a third floor, to a fifth floor. At the Prudential Center, all of fifty-two stories, I wound up getting him to the top, with the plan that he would then ride down on his own. Down I went and waited at the bottom; many minutes passed with no sign of Hank. Taking the elevator back up, there was still no Hank. I found him hiding a bit sheepishly behind a pay phone. Eventually, Hank was able to ride elevators without panicking, and we culminated our treatment with a lunch at the top of the Prudential Center. Later, I learned from a letter he sent me that he had removed his applications from midwestern colleges and wound up going to MIT.

This boy found his own help. Some adolescents are sufficiently self-aware and inspired to take action themselves and seek answers to their problems with social anxiety and panic. Some successfully confide in a counselor or admired teacher in school, who makes recommendations about productive steps to take. (Often, however, kids will go online and wind up in chatrooms, which typically tend to perpetuate inaccurate information. One teen tells another, "That therapy stuff is all bull. This is what I did, and here's what you should do…" The child is too likely to be guided in the wrong way.)

Most of the troubled teens we see have reached us after their parents became concerned enough to explore avenues of treatment. If in trying to help your adolescent you sense you have exhausted your ideas and your energy, and you're feeling depressed yourself about what seems to be an entrenched negative situation, consulting with a professional can be a wise move. Consider it if:

• Despite your best efforts at getting him out, connecting him with other kids, making the phone calls and following through, he's still resistant to even leaving the house.

• He seems perpetually sad, or gives any indication that he wishes he were never born.

• His avoidance has been going on for a long time.

• He resents all suggestions of change and says "no" to everything.

• He persistently denies that anything is wrong. (I've had many cases in which the teen says, "I'm perfectly happy. Why do you think I'm not? I don't really like other people, that's all," and meanwhile, he isn't bathing, looks like a mess, never smiles.)

• The problem displays itself in all contexts; he's not able to communicate with others at home, in school, in casual encounters.

Having a good assessment from a mental health professional can go a long way. Make sure you're not missing something, another disorder, perhaps, that interferes with your adolescent's ability to adopt these strategies. In the following chapter, you'll see suggestions about how to find help.

Parents can be great cheerleaders in getting kids going, but if the adolescent really doesn't want to attempt any of the activities I've outlined here, if his motivation is extremely low, it's probably not time to navigate the situation alone but to seek advice or treatment from an informed source.

IV

SPECIAL CONSIDERATIONS

CHAPTER 12

Growing Up Brave Through the Years

Finding Professional Help, Using Medications, Maintaining Progress

In the previous chapters, I have talked about children "getting better." So what does getting better look like? Should you expect that after following the suggestions in this book your child will not be anxious anymore?

We say that if anxious behavior has decreased to a place where it's manageable, that child is getting better. Now that you are aware of the normal and extreme expressions of anxiety, you will know when they are interfering with your child's day-to-day activities and you'll have good ideas for helping him cope with them. I sometimes use the analogy of adjusting the volume, not changing the station. The child with a naturally shy, inhibited temperament may not necessarily become the life of the party. The introvert doesn't necessarily turn into an extrovert. The worrier doesn't become a perpetually sunny optimist. He's the same child, except anxiety no longer rules his life.

Many parents are concerned about "setbacks," small glitches in forward progress. That word brings on a lot of negativity. When I gather further information and ask what happened over the previous week, I hear, "Well, he got nervous about soccer again. He didn't want to play, and he had been doing so great. This is a major setback." If the child is picking up on mom's worry or disappointment, he may respond in kind (*I'm not doing well, my panic is back*). We begin to see the avoidant behavior in other settings, not just on the soccer field.

In a true relapse or setback, the child starts to repeat a lot of the old patterns. But symptom fluctuations can happen in relation to situational stress—someone is sick, the family car got banged up in an accident—that brings on fears and makes him think danger is more likely. There are harder days and easier days. During difficult times you may see more anxiety; that's to be expected. And the children I'm talking about in this book might have a more anxious temperament than most, more prone to react to stress. Even if your child loses a little confidence, it's not gone for good.

Instead of worrying about a setback, point out to him, "You just had a hard day. Everyone has them. It's perfectly normal. We're going to start again tomorrow. I know you can do it." That kid is more likely to get back in the ring and keep trying to live up to the expectation of success. Tomorrow is going to be better. Most of the time, children tell us that with practice, challenges continue to be easier for them.

You might see progress in starts and stops, not in a steady forward line. Sometimes kids make a jump toward getting better, then fall back a bit, then make another jump. Some children will be able to take huge steps; for many, a little step at a time is what works best. As you're shaping behavior, pay attention to the little steps. I often suggest to parents that they write them out; make a master list of all the good coping the child has done, all the brave accomplishments achieved so far. He can look at his list when he's having a difficult time, and remember when he felt a little stronger; he feels more positive and knows, *Okay, I can get back and start again.*

Keep in mind that if your child has experienced anxiety problems, it's probably taken a long time for that pattern to develop, so it's a mistake to think that matters will be turned around overnight. Especially with some of the more severe cases, parents need to be patient.

And as important and influential as we are as parents, we still can't solve everything.

When Professional Help Is a Good Idea

Even with thoughtful parental intervention based on a deeper understanding of the nature of anxiety, some children continue to exhibit extreme responses to stressful situations. The more entrenched problems—obsessive-compulsive behavior that's been going on for a long time, for example—are often best treated by a professional who can begin to set the right course. If it seems that your child's quality of life isn't improving much, or he's upset about his own inability to control himself, or maybe the general family functioning is steadily undermined by his difficulties, even a few sessions—a booster—with a mental health professional might be useful.

If your child's teacher suggests seeing a psychologist, take it to heart. Children display behaviors in school, including anxiety, that they might not at home. Perhaps you can ask for a consult with the school counselor or social worker to assess what's going on and to see if extra recommendations are in order. Some parents elect to have a child's overall health checked in order to rule out any medical issues before considering therapy.

In some cases, involving an outside party can be a motivator for the child who thinks mom is just trying to run his life. (*I'm not going to do all this stuff that my mother wants, but I'll do it for this other person even though I don't know her very well.*) A therapist can also be a springboard to change for everyone, helping organize and integrate all family members so there's less blame and focus on the child.

If you're thinking professional input is a good idea, here are two considerations:

First, find a therapist who has been trained in delivering cognitive behavioral strategies, or in helping kids learn how to change their anxious thoughts and avoidant behaviors. I've described Cognitive Behavioral Therapy (CBT) as a skill-based, hands-on, evidence-supported approach. CBT is the frontline treatment for kids with excessive fear or anxiety. Use this term. In your first contact with a psychologist, ask, "What orientation do you use? Are you a cognitive behaviorally trained therapist?" If the answer is no, that individual shouldn't be your first choice for helping your anxious child.

Usually, treatment is relatively short-term, eight to sixteen sessions. You won't be in therapy for years; there's an end in sight, which is a nice aspect of CBT. It may take longer if the child has multiple issues, but for the most part the process is time-limited.

Second, find someone who specializes in working with children and adolescents. That's a skill in and of itself. This person will be cognizant of developmental stages, knowing what's normal at various ages. With adolescents, child training is less critical; the CBT psychologist can do what we call a downward extension of his approach with adults. But with a 6-year-old, there are specific techniques that work to keep the child engaged.

I'm often asked how to locate such an individual. Should you look in the phone book? Ask the pediatrician for recommendations? Ask your friend? Those might be perfectly adequate avenues. You can also research online professional organizations in the field, many of which include "find a therapist" listings arranged by state and city or zip code. Here are good sites to check out:

- **www.abct.org**

This website for the Association for Behavioral and Cognitive Therapies contains information about this kind of treatment and a directory of therapists around the United States.

- **www.adaa.org**

The Anxiety Disorders Association of America, a nonprofit organization, states that its mission is "to promote the prevention, treatment, and cure of anxiety disorders and to improve the lives of all people who suffer from them." The website includes a directory of therapists who specialize in treating anxiety disorders.

- **www.aboutourkids.org**

Sponsored by the New York University Child Study Center, this resource is dedicated to increasing awareness of child mental health issues and improving the treatment of child psychiatric illnesses.

- **www.childanxiety.net**

The Child Anxiety Network, an online resource for parents of children with anxiety, contains a directory of providers across the United States, as well as up-to-date information on anxiety disorders and their treatment.

- **www.apa.org/about/division/div53**

The Society of Clinical Child and Adolescent Psychology is a division of the website of the American Psychological Association.

Here is the online contact information for several outstanding child and adolescent anxiety disorders treatment centers:

- **www.bu.edu/card/clinical-services/child-programs**
Child and Adolescent Fear and Anxiety Treatment Program at the Center for Anxiety and Related Disorders at Boston University
- **www.anxietytreatmentnyc.org**
Columbia University Clinic for Anxiety and Related Disorders, in New York City
- **www.childanxiety.org**
Temple University Child and Adolescent Anxiety Disorders Clinic, providing services for children and teens in the Philadelphia area
- **www.casgroup.fiu.edu/capp**
Child Anxiety and Phobia Program at Florida International University in Miami
- **www.semel.ucla.edu/caap**
Child OCD, Anxiety, and Tic Disorders Program at UCLA
- **www.anxiouskids.org**
Providence-based Pediatric Anxiety Research Clinic located at Rhode Island Hospital and affiliated with Brown University medical school

Not everyone is near a specialty anxiety treatment center, though there are many individual therapists across the country who are trained in CBT techniques. In an area with less access, you have fewer choices. Sometimes it's worth traveling. If you live an hour away from a specialist with CBT training and ten minutes away from someone without it, go for the distant one. Ask if he can offer more intensive approaches, perhaps a two-hour rather than one-hour session.

What to Ask the Therapist

You don't have to grill this individual, but ask some questions to find out a little about his practice and how he works. Some therapists will be happy to have an initial phone consultation.

"Can you tell me about your experience with cognitive behavioral therapy?"

"What ages of children do you see?"

"Do you work with families? Do you include parents in the treatment? Would I be part of it?"

"How many sessions will it take before my child might show progress?"

The therapist obviously can't give you hard-and-fast promises. But in general, you want to get an idea of the course you may be embarking on. Depending on the child and on the nature of her disorder, great strides may be made in as few as three sessions, as you've read earlier in this book.

"Do you have groups for teens with social anxiety?"

If your concern is an adolescent with social phobia, group therapy is extremely helpful. In fact, it's probably the best way to treat this disorder. The nature of the therapy is itself a kind of exposure. At the start, kids aren't looking at one another, everyone is barely whispering, there's great awkwardness and discomfort all around. There are many turtles within their shells. By the end of therapy, the teens are talking; friendships have formed. In social phobia, the focus may be different for different children—a fear of blushing or making eye contact, perhaps, or of asking a question. But overall, the core fears are similar: rejection, embarrassment. And group support can be enormous. These young people just blossom.

"What hours are you available?"

The therapist may be highly experienced but have only

daytime hours. Some will see patients one night a week. Being flexible in the timing is important. If it's a pressing issue, you may choose to take your child out of school for the therapist's first session, though this at times can backfire. I've seen kids get anxious about missing school in order to go to a treatment for anxiety! However, if missing school is the only option in order to see a qualified CBT therapist, then you might weigh the costs-benefits equation. Often the benefits outweigh the costs.

Ask about fees and insurance.

Try it out for one session to receive an assessment. The therapist should conduct an initial intake to figure out the problems and then give you a sense of what the approach will be. He should review his conclusions with you and describe, without resorting to jargon, what was done—for example, what tests he gave your child, if any, and what they indicated. If you're ever handed an assessment report without comment, insist on an explanation.

If you begin treatment, remember that rapport takes time to build. Your child may be resistant at first, not ready to spill the beans the minute she walks into the therapist's office. After a couple of sessions, you may decide it's not a great personality match. It's all right to try someone new. Once you are under a therapist's care, it is that person's responsibility to try to help you if you want other referrals and to direct you to another professional who will take matters from there.

Medicating Your Child

I often talk to parents who say, "Our next step was going to be getting medication for our son." Just as often, I meet kids starting CBT who are already on medications. Their parents perhaps listened to a teacher or doctor, or even their own strong impulse, and decided to medicate their child to alleviate symptoms or behaviors. Some wanted the quick fix. Give the child something to help him out right now. Others are reluctant to put kids on drugs at any cost.

In many cases, I find that there is no need to rush to medicate. Frequently, when we help the child and his parent start to understand what the emotion of anxiety is all about and how the body works, and give the child some concrete coping skills, that information is enough to begin to calm down the entire family. However, that's not to say that medicating a child is always a bad idea. Psychopharmacological help might be wise if a child demonstrates persistent low mood or is suicidal, or when chronic and severe problems are apparent. Studies have shown that CBT in combination with medications sometimes works well for kids with significant distress and functional impairment. For many, therapy maintains gains longer than just taking a pill.

If you have any questions about the advisability of starting your child on medications, you can initiate a conversation with your psychologist, who will then refer you for a medication consult. You'll usually be directed to a psychiatrist, who can explain the various families of drugs, what they do, and the side effects associated with them. Sometimes pediatricians also will prescribe.

But it's important for the therapist to be in touch with the prescribing physician, so the two can share information and be aware of what's going on in treatment and medication. Coordinated care is the goal.

How to Keep the Progress Going

As I come to the end of *Growing Up Brave*, I've been thinking of the messages I would like to leave with you, a few last thoughts on helping to promote an autonomous and strong sense of self in your child. Here is what I hope you will take away from this book:

Reinforce the warm connection between the two of you—always, right through all her growing-up years (and beyond). Try to create some quiet times, just enjoying your child's company and her unique self, without judgment.

Maintain the positive reinforcement you've established. Usually anxious kids need to have small "getting brave" practices peppered here and there through their days. Encourage your child to keep challenging herself—not forever, but just until you see that she is able to master her tough situations.

Involve loved ones. Share some of the skills with other important people in her life—grandparents, dear uncles and aunts, a favorite teacher or coach. Children respond to consistency and predictability. All those who care for them can be supportive.

Celebrate successes all along. Celebrate even the tiny ones, the small steps. All the small steps lead to getting better.

Give yourself a pat on the back every now and then. As a psychologist, I am able to write with conviction about parenting actions that can be helpful. As a mother, I know how difficult it can be at times to implement them with your own child. I know the tug you may feel, wanting a child to be brave and wanting at the same time to relieve her distress, gather her close, and make the hard time go away. When you successfully navigate that line in the best interests of your child, you deserve a little praise yourself.

Over my years of practice, I've come to know hundreds of children with anxiety. So many of the kids I work with say, simply, that they wish their lives could be more fun. It's my hope that by using the strategies you've learned here, you will be able to help your child bring on more fun. Watch your child flourish, and enjoy the sight. There really are very few satisfactions greater than seeing a son or daughter no longer hampered by excessive fears, but reaching toward all the exciting possibilities that lie ahead.

After getting brave, one adolescent said to me, "My whole life has opened up. It's like freedom. I can do anything I want without anxiety getting the best of me." What could be better than that?

Acknowledgments

I would first like to thank Andrea Thompson, the writer who worked with me in developing *Growing Up Brave*, for her enthusiasm for this project, her professional and clear writing style, and her incredible ability to integrate and organize massive amounts of information. Her countless hours of hard work made it possible for this book to come together. I am also grateful for her relaxed, warm interpersonal style, which made it a pleasure to work with her.

I am especially appreciative of my agent, Eve Bridburg, for contacting me about writing this book, as well as for voicing her belief about how much potential it would have to help many people. She provided genuine encouragement through each step of the publishing process. I would also like to thank the entire team at the literary agency Zachary Shuster Harmsworth, who have all been helpful, from their enthusiasm to their time spent reading and editing drafts of the proposal.

A very special thank-you to my editor, Tracy Behar, and the entire team at Little, Brown. I felt Tracy's excitement for the book from the moment we agreed to work together. She and her colleagues have been supportive throughout every phase of publication, and I am grateful and proud to have had the opportunity to write my first parenting book with Little, Brown.

There are numerous professional mentors from whom I have been fortunate to learn throughout my career and whose ideas have very much shaped my own. Dr. David Barlow's hardworking style and continual drive to improve the lives of others through his research on the nature and treatment of anxiety disorders inspired me from the first days I began working at Boston University, and continues to inspire me in my clinical research career. I am grateful for Dr. Sheila Eyberg's expert mentorship during my years at the University of Florida. Dr. Eyberg and her colleagues' years of pioneering research developing Parent-Child Interaction Therapy provided a strong foundation for my work adapting the treatment to parents of anxious children.

I am also especially appreciative of several other professional mentors who are not only leaders in the field of child anxiety research and expert clinicians, but who have always supported my professional work: Dr. Thomas Ollendick, Dr. John Weisz, Dr. Anne Marie Albano, and my graduate mentor, Dr. Alice Friedman.

I would like to recognize numerous researchers for their outstanding and significant work that has collectively shaped our understanding of the nature, assessment, and treatment of child anxiety disorders. Their empirical work and writing have provided the foundation for many of the evidence-based cognitive-behavioral skills that I describe in *Growing Up Brave*. I am grateful for the work of Dr. Philip Kendall, Dr. Ronald Rapee, Dr. Bruce Chorpita, Dr. Jennifer Hudson, Dr. Wendy Silverman, Dr. John Piacentini, and Dr. John March, among countless others. The chapter on sleep in anxious youth is based on the pioneering work of many pediatric sleep experts, including Dr. Jodi Mindell, Dr. Judy Owens, and Dr. Candice Alfano. I am excited to have been able to integrate some of the relevant work on pediatric sleep into a book on child anxiety.

For the past twelve years, I have had the opportunity to direct the Child and Adolescent Fear and Anxiety Treatment Program at the Center for Anxiety and Related Disorders (CARD) at Boston University. I feel grateful to have the opportunity to work in such an internationally recognized specialty center for anxiety disorders, alongside outstanding colleagues who are each moving the field of anxiety research and treatment forward in substantial and meaningful ways. I am also especially appreciative of the outstanding and talented graduate students and staff in the Child and Adolescent Fear and Anxiety Treatment Program who help us daily in providing state-of-the-art treatment for children with anxiety disorders and their families, as well as helping us conduct meaningful clinical research. They have all experienced the very heart of the material in this book—witnessing children with anxiety disorders getting better. I am especially grateful to Dr. Jonathan Comer and Dr. Jami Furr for being such incredible collaborators and colleagues. A warm thank-you to Dr. Lisa Smith and Bonnie Brown, RN, for their continual support and encouragement throughout the years.

I also wish to thank the people who are at the core of the material in *Growing Up Brave*—the children and families with whom I have worked clinically as well as those who have participated in our research projects. Their contributions have made a difference in furthering our knowledge of effective child anxiety treatments, and they are greatly appreciated.

Above all, I would like to thank my friends and family for their collective enthusiasm for this project. The support I have received daily from my husband, Dr. John Otis, has quite simply made this book happen. A huge thank-you to Dr. Christina Hardway, Allyson Krause, Jeanine Maresca, Dr. Kamila White Bruce, Kimberly Glenn, Brad Seamon, Dr. Jackie Kloss, and especially Deborah and Michael Pincus, whose invaluable daily support has also substantially contributed to this book. I would like to gratefully acknowledge my parents, Dr. Laraine Pincus and Arnold Pincus, who modeled for me from an early age how to be unconditionally compassionate and who have supported me in every stage of my life. And last, thank you to my children for helping to teach me the most about how to parent. My hope is that the material in this book will help them and countless other children grow up brave.

Notes

1. A. Bandura, "Self-efficacy," in *Encyclopedia of Human Behavior*, edited by V. S. Ramachaudran (New York: Academic Press, 1994), vol. 4, 71–81. Reprinted in *Encyclopedia of Mental Health*, edited by H. Friedman (San Diego: Academic Press, 1998).
2. D. H. Barlow, *Anxiety and Its Disorders: The Nature and Treatment of Anxiety and Panic*, 2nd edition (New York: Guilford Press, 2002).
3. J. L. Hudson and R. M. Rapee, "Parent-Child Interactions and Anxiety Disorders: an Observational Study," in *Behaviour Research and Therapy* (2001): 39(12), 1411–1427.
4. J. L. Hudson, J. S. Comer, and P. C. Kendall, "Parental Responses to Positive and Negative Emotions in Anxious and Nonanxious Children," in *Journal of Clinical Child and Adolescent Psychology* (2008): 37/2, 303–313.
5. S. M. Eyberg and E. A. Robinson, "Parent-child Interaction Training: Effects on Family Functioning," in *Journal of Clinical Child Psychology* (1982): 11, 130–137.
6. C. B. McNeil and T. Hembree-Kigin, *Parent-Child Interaction Therapy*, 2nd edition (New York: Springer, 2010).
7. D. B. Pincus, J. T. Ehrenreich, L. Santucci, and S. M. Eyberg, "The Implementation of Modified Parent-Child Interaction Therapy for Youth with Separation Anxiety Disorder," in *Cognitive and Behavioral Practice* (2008): 15/2, 118–125.
8. R. M. Chase and D. B. Pincus, "Sleep-related Problems in Children and Adolescents with Anxiety Disorders," in *Behavioral Sleep Medicine* (2011): 9(4), 224–236.

Index

game of catch, 148
generalized anxiety disorder
    (GAD), 40–41, 103, 135, 144
generalized social phobia, 46
graduated extinction, 112
group therapy, 223, 251

hyperventilation, 233–34

I Can Relax! (CD), 159, 160–68,
    232–33
icky scavenger hunt, 178
imitation, in five-minutes-a-day
    time, 80
infants, normal fears of, 32–33
inferiority-anxiety-avoidance
    patterns, 22
interoceptive exposure exercise,
    151–53, 156–59, 157, 217, 228
intrusive parents, 57–59, 83

labels
    labeled praise, 79–80, 111, 176,
        186, 195
    role of, 48–49
large or unfamiliar objects, 32–33
learning disabilities, 20–21
loud noises, 32

magical thinking, 43–44, 137–39
medications
    advice on, 7, 252–53
    effectiveness of, 4
    side effects of, 6
middle-school-age children,
    normal fears of, 36
mind reading, anxious thoughts,
    132–34
misbehavior. *See also* oppositional
    behavior
    in five-minutes-a-day time,
        96–98
modeling
    anxious parents and, 61–63
    cognitive restructuring and, 149
    non-nervous behavior and, 31
    positive behaviors, 177–79

monitoring, bedtime-monitoring
    checklist, 108–9, 111, 117
moral issues, adolescents' fears
    concerning, 37
motivation
    adolescence and, 241
    Bravery Ladder and, 187,
        194–95, 196
    professional help and, 248
    skills-based treatment and, 25
motivational interviewing, 115

naps, 107
New York University Child Study
    Center, 249
normal behavior
    anxiety as normal emotion, 5,
        11–12, 14–16, 27–29, 31–37, 38,
        39, 94, 153, 245
    anxiety disorders compared to, 7

obsessive-compulsive disorder
    bedtime and sleep management
        and, 103
    magical thinking and, 43–44,
        137–39
    modeling positive behaviors and,
        177–79
    professional help for, 247
oppositional behavior
    adolescence and, 236
    anxious thoughts and, 137–38
    bedtime and sleep management
        and, 109–11
oppositional defiant disorder, 74
overly reassuring parents, 59–61
overt avoidance, 171

panic attacks. *See also* panic
    disorder
    adolescence and, 85, 217, 218
    Bravery Ladders and, 198–99,
        209
    catastrophic thinking and,
        230, 231
    cycle of anxiety and, 122
    fears of, 17, 22, 45

play therapy, 24
practice, Bravery Ladder, 187,
   198–200
praise
   adolescence and, 86, 235–36
   bedtime and sleep management
      and, 109–13
   Bravery-Directed Interaction
      and, 187
   five-minutes-a-day time, 79–80,
      91, 92, 96, 186
   labeled praise, 79–80, 111, 176,
      186, 195
   reinforcement and, 176–77
preschool children, normal fears of,
   33–35
present moment, brave
   behavior, 14
probability overestimation
   anxious thoughts and, 130,
      132, 142
   playing detective with,
      142–44, 230
professional help
   benefits of, 7, 247–50
   questions to ask therapist, 251–52
   specialists in children and
      adolescents, 248–49
   websites of professional
      organizations, 249–50
progressive muscle relaxation
   adolescence and, 116, 217–18,
      232–34
   benefits of, 159, 169
   exposure therapy and, 185
   hungry at the beach, 165
   I Can Relax!, 167–68
   making lemonade, 162–63
   relaxing place, 160–61
   relax your face, 164–65
   strong, tall tree, 166–67
   taking deep breaths, 160
   taking a nap, 165–66
   turtle and the stream, 163–64
   worry train, 161
psychotropic drugs. *See*
   medications

public speaking, 145–47, 183–84,
   210–11

questions, in five-minutes-a-day
   time, 77–78

real chances exploration, 144
real-world dangers, 35
reflection, in five-minutes-a-day
   time, 80, 91, 186
reinforcement, 172–77. *See also*
   rewards
relational aggression, in middle-
   school-age children, 36
relaxation exercises. *See also*
   progressive muscle relaxation
   adolescence and, 116
   sleep hygiene and, 107
resistance
   adolescence and, 226, 227, 240
   Bravery Ladder and, 187, 195–98
   professional help and, 252
response bursts, 212–13
rewards
   adolescence and, 114
   bedtime-monitoring checklist
      and, 108, 109, 117
   Bravery Ladder and, 187, 188,
      189, 190, 191–94, 195, 200,
      204, 214–16
   guidelines for, 193–94, 254
   parent-child interaction and, 61,
      94, 112, 143–44, 148, 187
   reinforcement and, 174–77
Reward Store, 191–94
routines. *See also* bedtime and sleep
   management
   benefits of, 102–3
   for confident behavior, 7
rumination, 55

safety person, 229, 236
say the secret word, 148–49
school failure, in elementary-
   school-age children, 36
selective mutism, 111
self-efficacy

About the Author

Donna B. Pincus, PhD, is an associate professor and the director of the Child and Adolescent Fear and Anxiety Treatment Program at the Center for Anxiety and Related Disorders at Boston University. Dr. Pincus is one of the nation's leading experts in the diagnosis and treatment of child anxiety disorders and has helped hundreds of children and families overcome anxiety disorders and return to healthy functioning. She received her PhD in clinical psychology from Binghamton University and completed her clinical internship at the University of Florida Health Sciences Center, with a child-pediatric specialty.

Dr. Pincus has focused her clinical research career on the development of new treatments for child anxiety disorders. She has been the recipient of several research grants from the National Institute of Mental Health to develop innovative treatments for early childhood separation anxiety disorder and adolescent panic disorder and has published numerous scholarly articles, chapters, books, and treatment manuals on the assessment and treatment of child and adolescent anxiety disorders. In addition to her involvement with research, she trains and mentors doctoral students at Boston University and treats children and adults with anxiety disorders with evidence-based cognitive-behavioral therapy.

Dr. Pincus has also dedicated part of her career to sharing information about effective cognitive-behavioral treatments for anxiety disorders to the public. She is the editor and creator of the Child Anxiety Network (www.childanxiety.net), an online resource for parents, teachers, psychologists, and other professionals who want accurate information and resources on child anxiety. She is an active public speaker and has given numerous workshops and seminars on child anxiety to parents, teachers, students, and health-care professionals around the world. Dr. Pincus's work with children and adolescents with anxiety disorders has been featured on national media shows and networks, including *Good Morning America*, *20/20*, *Today*, Lifetime Television, and National Geographic Television.